UNDERSTANDING
CHIPPED
STONE TOOLS

PRINCIPLES OF ARCHAEOLOGY

ADVISORY EDITORS

Robert L. Bettinger, *University of California, Davis*
Gary M. Feinman, *The Field Museum, Chicago, Illinois*

A PRIMER ON MODERN–WORLD ARCHAEOLOGY
Charles E. Orser, Jr.

REGIONAL SETTLEMENT DEMOGRAPHY IN ARCHAEOLOGY
Robert D. Drennan, C. Adam Berrey, Christian E. Peterson

APPLIED ZOOARCHAEOLOGY: Five Case Studies
Steve Wolverton, Lisa Nagaoka, Torben C. Rick

THE ARCHAEOLOGY OF ANCIENT CITIES
Glenn R. Storey

A PRIMER ON CHIEFS AND CHIEFDOMS
Timothy Earle

UNDERSTANDING CHIPPED STONE TOOLS
Brian Hayden

UNDERSTANDING
CHIPPED
STONE TOOLS

BRIAN HAYDEN

Simon Fraser University (Burnaby) and
University of British Columbia (Vancouver)
British Columbia, Canada

ELIOT WERNER PUBLICATIONS, INC.
CLINTON CORNERS, NEW YORK

Library of Congress Cataloging-in-Publication Data

Names: Hayden, Brian, author.
Title: Understanding chipped stone tools / Brian Hayden.
Description: Clinton Corners, New York : Eliot Werner Publications, Inc.,
    2022. | Series: Principles of archaeology | Includes bibliographical
    references.
Identifiers: LCCN 2021046141 (print) | LCCN 2021046142 (ebook) |
ISBN
    9781734281866 (paperback) | ISBN 9781734281873 (epub) | ISBN
    9781734281880 (pdf)
Subjects: LCSH: Stone implements. | Tools, Prehistoric.
Classification: LCC GN799.T6 H39 2022 (print) | LCC GN799.T6
(ebook) | DDC 930.1/2—dc23/eng/20220103

ISBN-10: 1-7342818-6-3
ISBN-13: 978-1-7342818-6-6

Printed in the United States of America

To the memory of my father, who first encouraged
me to become an archaeologist

PREFACE

This book distills insights from the better part of my career, which has been spent trying to understand the mysteries of stone tools: how they were made, what they were used for, what variations are meaningful, and how they fit into the cultures that generated them. In pursuing this quest, I went to the Australian deserts to work with Aboriginals who remembered making and using stone tools; I went to France to study with François Bordes; and I learned how to make stone tools and use them to work hides, chop wood, make spears and bone awls, and undertake many other projects. I have obtained a fairly good grasp of many of the fundamental aspects of stone tools, and I would like to pass along these aspects to readers keen to know about stone technology.

My goal in this book is to convey—in a basic and simple way—the perspective that I have found most useful for dealing with stone tools. The study of chipped stone tools is sometimes viewed as an arcane field that can only be understood by the most serious devotees, and is often dealt with superficially by the least informed. What I want to present is an engaging way of looking at stone tools, tools designed to solve basic problems. And to understand these problems and how stone tools were used to solve them, it is necessary to engage with the traditional world, to know first hand what it is like to make a spear using stone tools or an awl or a shell bead. Understanding stone technology is best done on an experiential basis, not simply from reading books. And this is what makes it engaging and fun. Learning by doing is far more effective than learning through reading. It makes connections to the real world and can be a lifelong source of satisfaction.

This book is mainly for students and others who are just setting out to explore what stone tools are all about—people who want to see if studying stone tools is what they want to pursue. It is meant to engage your interest rather than provide all the details you need to know about lithic technology. Detailed studies can come later and there are many other books that explain in much more detail the mechanics of flaking stone, typologies of tools, ways of measuring stone tools, the characteristics of debitage and core reduction, determining geological types of stone used, use-wear traces, residue analysis, and many other facets. This book is different. It is a conceptual approach focused on the user's decisions in the design of tools and what stone tools were used for. I hope you get some enjoyment out of a number of the exercises, and I hope you obtain a good grounding in understanding how stone tools were made, why certain techniques were used for flaking, and how stone could be modified to solve specific problems.

I will forever be in the debt of everyone who has taught me about lithics, and consider myself to have been very lucky for the good mentoring and productive interactions I have had with gifted individuals—whether in academia or in native settlements. These individuals are far too numerous to list but François Bordes, Errett Callahan, Don Crabtree, Jeffrey Flenniken, Johan Kamminga, Maxine Kleindienst, and Jim Riggs stand out.

I am very grateful to Eliot Werner for this opportunity to present my views on lithic analysis and pull together a number of disparate pieces of research that I have carried out over the years. I also wish to thank the students and colleagues who collaborated on the research mentioned in this book. Finally, except where noted the photographs in the book were taken by me.

CONTENTS

CHAPTER 1

PERSPECTIVES ON LITHICS

Stone tools are perplexing when you first look at them—a jumbled collection of sharp-edged chunks of stone with no rhyme or reason to their existence except for the occasional arrowhead or spearhead. Which pieces were the equivalent of industrial waste and which were useful? What can we learn from analyzing lithics? A lot more than you might initially suspect.

Stone tools are the Stone Age equivalent of modern plastics: they don't decay and they litter the landscape wherever there were people. There is even "microdebitage" in the landscape from producing stone tools. People just threw away stone tools and stone waste when they were done with them, no matter where they were. They have lasted for thousands, hundreds of thousands, and even millions of years. The Egyptians called stone the material of eternity. As one bumper sticker proclaimed at a conference in England, "Love is fleeting but stone tools are forever."

PERSPECTIVES:
OLD, NEW, AND FROM THE BOTTOM UP

When first encountered by people plowing their fields, stone artifacts were mysterious things thought to have been produced by lightning strikes shattering rocks. "Thunder stones," they called them. Since the time of Christian Thomson, who identified the Stone Age as a technological stage of cultural evolution in 1820 and who employed the concept of evolution a half-century before Darwin, archaeologists have used experimentation, use-wear analysis, ethnographic observations, replication, tool designs, and residue examination to gradually develop an understanding of how stone tools were made and what many types of stone tools were used for.

1

This book does not cover details about flintknapping techniques, mineralogy of stones, ground stone tools, or fracture mechanics. These are specialized topics best dealt with in separate works. Rather, it represents a somewhat different approach to analyzing chipped stone assemblages than traditional books. Most books on lithic analysis begin with describing types of stone, the mechanics of stone fracture, and the various types of stone reduction. They include an examination of some tool types, discussions of use-wear, and sometimes expositions about mobility effects or a few other factors that affect assemblages. They represent a top-down analytical perspective typical of geological or paleontological approaches to natural phenomena that emphasize mineral components and structure and treat artifacts like fossils to be described, measured, and placed in appropriate categories or understood in terms of their environments.

What I propose is to employ the viewpoints of the makers and users to approach chipped stone tools from a more holistic, bottom-up framework—an agent-based approach if you like, and one that I have used elsewhere to understand feasting and ritual behavior. Perhaps the most distinctive cognitive feature in human evolution has been the amazing ability of humans to solve problems in innovative and effective ways by employing highly developed conceptual skills in logic, causality, memory, foresight, and imagination. To undertake lithic analysis from this perspective, I have found the conceptual framework provided by design theory to be uniquely suited to the goal of understanding stone tools.

The next chapter describes exactly what this entails. The result of using this approach is that a broad range of constraints need to be identified that affect stone tool decisions and solutions. These include not only mobility constraints but also time constraints, procurement costs, effectiveness and efficiency of alternate solutions, quantities being processed, and transport aids—as well as social and other constraints. Design theory integrates them all.

WHAT DO YOU WANT TO FIND OUT?

What do you want to know about stone tools? This question is of fundamental importance in undertaking any analysis, whether of stone tools or anything else. Merely recording observations is a limitless and meaningless task. Analysis needs to be structured by things that you—or whoever is directing a project—want to know. What preoccupies me is what people were doing with stone tools, how stone artifacts got where they were found, and how they relate to social aspects in the past. But other people have different priorities. They may want to know what cultures or time periods stone tools represent, what interactions and exchanges took place with other groups, how mobile groups were, or how stone tools could be used to impress others. And indeed none of these topics are mutually exclusive. Sometimes analysis includes recording observations that can be used to deal with a number of different questions like cultural groupings, the age of artifacts, past exchanges, and the use of tools. But to engage in good analysis you should be aware of which observations are useful for dealing with specific kinds of questions (see Chapter 7).

If you are doing analysis for a consulting company, their "rote" kinds of inquiry are usually dictated by bureaucratic or client terms of reference. The problem that government agencies want to solve is how to standardize reports so that they are useful for managing cultural resources. This is an administrative problem usually involving lithic remains from different time periods and different cultural groups. To standardize recording the required typology of these agencies usually reflects time and culturally sensitive artifact types, as well as general assemblage descriptions that incorporate obvious use categories like "projectile points" and "grinding stones."

The objectives of these standardized typologies haven't changed much from the typologies developed in the first century of archaeological research—that is, to identify how old assemblages are and what cultural groups produced them. Indeed, for many archaeologists the term "typology" implies these purposes in the analysis of stone tools. In Europe this approach was borrowed from historical geologists (paleontologists) who tried to determine the kind of animals that existed in the past and the age of geological layers from the different types of bones occurring in the sediments. Stone tools were just another kind of physical remain, or fossil, to be used in the same way. In the last fifty years, archaeology and paleontology have expanded the range of issues being addressed—from sociopolitical organizations to rituals, social identities, domestication, dynamics of change, agency, and much more. We need different kinds of analyses to address these different kinds of questions.

EXPERIENTIAL AND EXPERIMENTAL ARCHAEOLOGY

In order to understand the strategies employed in the past, it is above all important to indulge in what I refer to as experimental and experiential archaeology. This consists of learning how to knap flint or stone and how to use a variety of stone tools to accomplish basic tasks like making spears or baskets. I am convinced that understanding how to make *and use* stone tools is pivotal to understanding how to analyze stone tools. This approach was pioneered by archaeologists like Errett Callahan and Jeffrey Flenniken. At the end of my own classes on lithics, we always had a three-day "field trip" that included camping out in the wilderness. The only things students were allowed to bring were their clothes, a sleeping bag, and one sandwich—as well as any piece of technology they had made themselves with stone tools.

In sum, this book charts an ambitious direction for analyzing lithic assemblages and provides the theoretical underpinnings for making sense of what stone tools represent in behavioral and cultural terms. If you want to seriously pursue the analysis of stone tools, my advice is to start making and using them and to read as many ethnographies as you can that involve traditional technologies—especially the use of stone tools. Even if people use metal tools today in traditional tasks, try to figure out what kinds of stone tools could have done those same tasks and how critical the tasks were in earlier societies. At one level or another, ethnographic analogy and ethnoarchaeology are indispensable for the interpretation of stone tools, but they need to be used wisely (see Chapter 9). Experiment around. Find out what works and what doesn't. Try to cut off a tree branch with stone tools. Trample some flakes to see what kind of damage results. Try to make a shell bead or a bone awl. The list is extensive but you will learn a great deal and have fun doing it.

MY BACKGROUND

To provide some appreciation of where I am coming from, it may be worth knowing that I have always been intrigued by what stone tools five thousand, fifty thousand, or five hundred thousand years old were used for. This was the big unsolved mystery for me. At the time it seemed to me that if archaeologists couldn't tell what stone tools were used for, then they couldn't say much about what was happening in Stone Age societies or what those societies were like. This may not be strictly true today but there is still a good deal of truth in it.

I spent a year at the University of Bordeaux studying with François Bordes, who showed us how to make Upper Paleolithic types of tools like laurel leaves and blades and let us try our hand at doing the same. I looked through the drawers and boxes in his collections of Mousterian stone artifacts and learned how to identify what had been done to flakes to modify them as tools (the topic for Chapter 4). But he never ventured to interpret what notches or scrapers or denticulates had been used for, and what those tools had been used for always intrigued me.

So when I returned to the University of Colorado and took a class on Australian ethnography, I was fascinated to watch silent black-and-white films made by Norman Tindale in the 1930s that showed Aborigines making and using stone tools. The scenes were frustratingly short and it was impossible to see the details of the stone tools in order to compare them with Mousterian types of tools or any others. Recourse to the early published accounts of stone tool use also did not provide the kind of detail that was needed to interpret prehistoric tools. Hence, when I entered graduate school, I applied to the Fulbright Foundation to study the manufacture and use of stone tools among the Australian Aborigines. In the 1970s there were still a few groups with members who had used stone tools in their youth. The result was very satisfying for me with a great many insights, not least of which was finally understanding what notches and denticulates were used for (Figure 1.1). I was also extremely fortunate to have Peter White as a sponsor, for he had documented in great detail the manufacture and use of stone tools in New Guinea. We had a lot of interests in common.

Years later I discovered that there were still individuals in the Maya highlands who were making grinding stones by using stone choppers to chip away at blocks of vesicular basalt (Figure 1.2). As part of the long-term excavations at the Keatley Creek site in British Columbia, I directed the analysis of the very large chipped stone assemblage from the site and checked all the identified tools. I also taught classes on the analysis of stone tools, including how to make them. Over the years I have come

Figure 1.1. Ethnoarcharchaeology can provide important insights into stone tool uses. What notched stones were used for was a mystery to me until I saw one being used by an Aboriginal Australian from the Western Desert for sharpening the wooden tip of a spear.

Figure 1.2. Another intriguing question is what stone tools prehistoric Maya used to cut the limestone blocks, stelae, and basalt metates. I was amazed to find this stoneworking tradition still alive in the Guatemalan highlands. Ramon Ramos is shown here using a chopping shaped tool to remove flakes of vesicular basalt in roughing out a grinding stone. The flake he removed can be seen falling away from the metate block.

to know a fair amount about stone tools and how to approach them. I would therefore like to pass on some of these insights to readers of this primer. For more details about the nuts and bolts—or tools and debitage—of lithic analysis, there are a number of other good books available.

ORGANIZATION OF THIS BOOK

The next two chapters will be devoted to establishing an overall conceptual structure for analyzing stone tools. The conceptual structure I have found most useful is design theory. Following this, in Chapter 4 we will look at what modifications are most commonly observed that indicate flakes were used as tools. Then Chapter 5 discusses the various strategies used to reduce raw stone material into tools. Chapter 6 presents a number of design considerations that can affect the nature of tools, such as reliability and maintainability. Typologies of tools are also discussed in Chapter 6. Changes in resharpening strategies are the topic of Chapter 7. As an example of what a lithic analysis is like for a site from a design perspective, Chapter 8 uses the housepit assemblages from Keatley Creek, British Columbia—where I have worked for more than three decades. And Chapter 9 discusses overall perspectives, suggestions, and prospects for doing lithic analysis. Exercises are provided after many chapters to help understand key concepts or perspectives and to begin involving readers in experiential archaeology.

EXERCISE

The goal of this exercise is to use a piece of stone to shape the end of a piece of wood into a point as if it were a spear or digging stick. First, find a branch or sapling of hardwood (leafy) tree that is two centimeters in diameter. Cut it using a saw. Now go to the nearest stream with cobbles in it and try to find stone material that you think will be able to cut wood. Also find a hammerstone. Try to remove a flake. What kind of stone did you choose? What kind of stone could break so that it had a sharp edge? What did it look like? What size pebble or cobble was best for the removal of a flake? Look up the geological definition of pebble and cobble. What shape was best for removing a flake? Assuming you succeeded, has your opinion changed of the mental and physical capabilities of early hominins (like Australopithecines) who made choppers on cobbles?

Once you have succeeded in removing several flakes, use the sharp edge of your cobble tool to shape your branch into a point and then refine it with a flake you have removed so that the point could be used for spearing an animal or digging roots out of the ground. How long did it take? How effective were your tools? Did you try any other flakes or materials to see which worked best? What edge angles seemed to work best? What kinds of materials worked best (describe what the rock was like)?

If you do not live near a stream with suitable rocks for this exercise, you can use something ceramic like an old thick dinner plate (not your mother's fine china!), pieces of a discarded toilet bowl, or any other kind of thick ceramic. Just break it up with a hammerstone and use different edges to see what sizes and edges are most effective.

ADDITIONAL READINGS

Barker, Wayne, and Brian Hayden. 1981. *Western Desert Woomera* (16 millimeter film). Australian Institute of Aboriginal Studies, Canberra. This is one of the very rare films that exist showing how stone tools were made and used by hunter-gatherers. Wayne Barker and I made it in the Australian Western Desert. If you can get to see a copy, it is an eye-opening ten minutes.

Callahan, Errett. 1994. *Primitive Technology: Practical Guidelines for Making Stone Tools, Pottery, Basketry, Etc. the Aboriginal Way.* Piltdown Productions, Lynchburg, Virginia. Callahan epitomizes the experiential approach to understanding traditional technology—that is, understanding by making and using technology. He is one of the best flint-knappers in the world and established the Society of Primitive Technology and the journal *Primitive Technology*, which the society publishes and has lots of useful insights. This thin, 25-page booklet is a useful primer.

Flenniken, J. Jeffrey. 1981. *Replicative Systems Analysis of the Lithic Artifacts from the Hoko River Archaeological Site.* Reports of Investigations No. 89, Laboratory of Anthropology, Washington State University, Pullman. Flenniken is another experiential archaeologist who pioneered the understanding of hunter-gatherer stone technologies—especially how small flakes were made, hafted, and used for butchering salmon. This is a classic study.

Hayden, Brian. 1979. *Paleolithic Reflections: Lithic Technology and Ethnographic Excavation Among Australian Aborigines.* Australian Institute of Aboriginal Studies, Canberra. This is a summary of the ethnoarchaeological research that I conducted with aborigines in the Australian Western Desert. It documents in great detail how stone tools were made, hafted, and used traditionally. It is a unique study for hunter-gatherer stone technology and provides special insights into the resharpening strategies for tools and the use of notches.

Hayden, Brian. 1987. Traditional Metate Manufacturing in Guatemala Using Chipped Stone Tools. In *Lithic Studies Among the Contemporary Highland Maya*, edited by Brian Hayden, pp. 8–119. University of Arizona Press, Tucson. As far as I know, this is the *only* study of how grinding stones were traditionally made using stone tools. The encounter with one of the few remaining practitioners of this Maya tradition was totally unexpected and serendipitous. There was no hint anywhere that such stone tool users still existed in the Maya Highlands.

Kamminga, Johan, and Brian Cotterell. 1990. *Mechanics of Pre-Industrial Technology: An Introduction to the Mechanics of Ancient and Traditional Material Culture.* Cambridge University Press, Cambridge, UK. Kamminga extended his experimental investigation into flaking mechanics and other prehistoric domains by teaming up with an engineering materials specialist and producing a milestone treatise based on engineering principles and experiments.

Wescott, David (editor). 1999. *Primitive Technology: A Book of Earth Skills.* Gibbs-Smith Publishers, Salt Lake City, Utah. A selective compilation of some of the most useful articles and illustrations from the journal *Primitive Technology* that exemplify the experiential approach to traditional technology. While most of the entries do not deal with stone technology, all involve the making and use of traditional items, and it is useful to think about which of these items would have required stone tools—and what kinds of stone tools—to make them.

CHAPTER 2

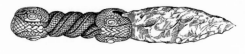

DESIGN THEORY

I first learned about design theory from Maxine Kleindienst when I studied at the University of Toronto. As early as 1975, she was publishing articles strongly advocating the use of design theory for analyzing Paleolithic stone tools. The major advantage of using design theory is that it provides a systematic framework for taking into account *all* the important factors that go into developing tools. This includes a number of key cultural aspects involving mobility, scheduling, labor, and social goals.

Design theory was developed by engineers to improve the design of machinery and industrial items. But it is a system that works equally well for understanding the design of traditional tools—whether of stone, bone, wood, clay, or anything else. It is a system that explicates the way tools were made and used. And whether or not we are conscious of making decisions about all the constraints involved in solving the technological problems we face, it is a system that we intuitively and implicitly use all the time. Often we have worked out familiar solutions to problems so that our solutions just seem to occur naturally to us.

This chapter provides an overview of design theory, but if you are interested in the details, see the additional readings. In Chapter 3 we will see how design theory can be applied to stone tools.

STEPS IN DESIGN ANALYSIS

The starting point of design theory analysis from an engineering perspective is (1) the identification of a basic problem to be solved (as opposed to starting with the stone tool itself). Obviously, previous analyses of stone tools (as well as analyses of other archaeological materials augmented by ethnographic observations) help determine what the basic problems were in the past. For example, most hunter-gatherers faced challenges of how to dig roots out of the ground, how to catch or kill prey, how to create shelter, how to transport quantities of seeds or berries or water, and how to protect themselves against the elements. From archaeological evidence we can also establish that more complex hunter-gatherers or other complex cultures needed to solve additional problems, such as how to cut down fairly large trees for making ocean-going canoes or building multifamily structures. Thus adopting a design perspective involves an evolving back-and-forth dialectic between inferences about what specific tools were used for and inferences about the problems people had to solve.

Once we identify the kinds of specific problems that had to be solved, the next step (2) in analysis is to identify the "constraints" that determine acceptable design solutions. After this we can (3) determine what kinds of solutions were available to solve the problems. This results in (4) an evaluation of the costs or benefits of each alternative solution. This kind of analysis requires a consideration of trade-offs that usually lead to the identification of a number of more or less optimal solutions, as well as identifying the most important factors that influenced prehistoric technologists' decisions.

Ultimately, a lithic assemblage needs to be examined in order to identify the tools that *could* have been used to solve particular problems. This provides a working model to be tested. Then (5) tools need to be assessed to determine their function through various means.

- Use-wear analysis.
- Ethnographic analogies.
- Context (spatial associations or haftings as with microblades in sickles or antler projectile points).
- Edge angles.
- Size and weight.
- Raw material.
- Residues.
- Experiments.
- Greater in-depth morphological/mechanical analysis.

The design analyses (6) need to explain why types of materials, reduction strategies, resharpening strategies, and discard patterns were associated with particular solutions to specific problems.

In a sense we have to work backward—or at least backward and forward—in the design process: unlike industrial engineers, we not only work from the problem to the optimal tool solutions, but also from the tool to the problem, and we have to deal with all the constraints along the way. It is a daunting undertaking that lays out futures for entire careers, but it's not necessary to solve every part. Just working out one or two of the constraints of certain tool designs can be a major contribution to the discipline and our understanding of stone tools. However, it is important to be aware of how your analysis—no matter how small—fits into a larger interpretive framework such as this.

Another approach widely used by French prehistorians is the analysis of what is referred to as the *chaîne opératoire* (literally "operational chain" or "operational sequence"). This usually consists of a detailed description of the sequence of steps involved in the production, use, and discard of an artifact. Although conceptually it can encompass a broad range of explanatory factors, in practice it differs from design theory in that it primarily describes manufacturing and kinematic processes without explaining why particular production strategies were adopted or the costs and benefits of various solutions.

DESIGN THEORY IN PRACTICE

So how does design theory work in practice? As an example that you may be familiar with, say that you are camping and have brought along a nice bottle of Belgian beer to drink around the fire—something you were really looking forward to enjoying. But you didn't realize that it wasn't a twist-top bottle and you didn't remember to bring a bottle opener. The problem, then, is how to open the one bottle of beer. Pause for a moment to think about how you would deal with this problem, or how you may have dealt with it in the past.

Constraints

There are numerous constraints that influence your choice of possible solutions.

Location and Mobility

What constraints does the location of this problem pose? How far do you need to go to get materials or tools? What kind of mobility is available (cars, bikes, canoes, walking) and how does this affect the costs and benefits of solutions?

Time and Scheduling

How much time do you have to devote to solving this problem? How much time are you willing to devote to it? You could hike or drive back to the nearest town to get a bottle opener. Alternatively, you could try to use other solutions, or even find other campers to see if they have a bottle opener.

Material Availability

You could expediently use materials that are immediately available. What materials come to mind? Some possibilities include using the back of a knife to pry the top off, or using the point to pry each individual crimp up in turn. You could use the end of a spoon or fork to pry. You could use the end of a shovel. I have seen a thick newspaper tightly folded and the tip of the fold used to pry off a cap. You could even use a sharp-edged stone, or if you are lithic savvy you could put a sharp edge on a stone! If none of these materials are available, I have seen people use their teeth or even their eye sockets to pop caps off. Finally, if you have a file or something to cut metal or plastic and a few pieces of plastic (credit cards, for example) or scrap metal plate or even a board of hard wood—even a thin piece of split firewood—you could create a simple bottle opener by carving or filing a hook into the edge of several plastic credit cards bunched together or file a hook into the piece of wood or metal. Do you have other suggestions? If none of these solutions are appealing, you could also simply use a stone to break off the top of the bottle.

What materials are actually available and can be used? Which have high costs compared with the benefits?

Effectiveness.

We now have an array of possible solutions. Which of them would you find adequately effective and which would be unacceptably effective?

Cultural Constraints

Which solutions would you reject because of cultural values—that is, solutions you find unpleasant due to your cultural values?

Risks

What risks are involved in the various solutions? Cuts, bruises, chipped teeth, glass shards in the beer?

Criticality

How critical is solving this problem to you? How much time and effort are you willing to put into solving it?

Technological Constraints

What technologies are available to use or to expediently adapt for use? What technological product are you capable of producing on your own?

Costs and Benefits

What are the relative costs (effort, time, risks) and benefits of the various solutions?

Design Considerations

You are now ready to choose your own design solution to this problem. You may want to take into consideration any risks or discomforts involved (getting cut, chipping teeth, hurting your hand), as well as the awkwardness of some solutions (the size of your opener, the ease of prehension, the likelihood of material failure or breakage, the edge angles involved), and similar design considerations.

Multiple Optimal Solutions

Is there just one single best solution for opening your bottle of beer, or are there several that you would be willing to try if the first choice did not work out? Design theory usually anticipates a number of relatively equal solutions to problems.

Implementation.

You are now ready to create a tool to open your bottle of beer, or to expediently use some material already at hand. What is your choice?

The Importance of Quantity

This is exactly the same process that traditional technologists go through when trying to deal with problems they encounter. If they are out camping and kill a rabbit for dinner but want to keep the skin for tanning, what would they use to prepare it if they had neglected to bring an end scraper or even any other flakes?

An important issue arises with both the beer bottle and rabbit skin, a question that very few archaeologists ever mention or think about: *quantity*. If you have only one item—one bottle, one animal—as your problem to deal with, you will probably be willing to put up with many less-than-optimal solutions that are difficult or uncomfortable to use, take undue time, effort, or risk, or that might barely work but do get the job done. How would your choice of solutions change for opening beer bottles if you were at a large party in charge of opening hundreds of bottles of beer, but you had no bottle opener? How would a hunter's solution change for preparing hides if he or she had dozens of hides to process instead of just one small rabbit skin? Considering quantity may give you a key insight into why specialized tools like end scrapers developed.

Rob Gargett and I looked into this a number of years ago. In our research design, we sought out a task or problem that would be analogous to a problem found among hunter-gatherers. We settled on an analysis of fish butchering. This was an especially good focus since there is such a range of fish processing on the British Columbian coast—from people who butcher a few fish per year as occasional anglers to large packing plants processing millions of fish per year. What we found was that people who infrequently caught and prepared fish used a single, all-purpose knife. But as the frequency of fish processing increased, efficiency became more important in each separate part of the processing so that more specialized kinds of knives were used for different sizes of fish and each task: heading, slitting, gutting, trimming (finning), steaking, and filleting. Thus people who caught and prepared 30–50 fish per year used only one type of knife; those who prepared two hundred kilograms of fish a day used four different types of knives; and those who prepared five hundred thousand kilograms of fish a day used five different types or sizes of knives. Our data also showed that knives used in butchering land mammals exhibited the same pattern.

This is a classic outcome in industrial design theory in which the higher cost of making or procuring specialized tools only becomes worth the required investment when the *total* efficiency saving that it provides surpasses the costs. And this only happens when volumes being processed reach critical crossover points. This is also an entirely expectable outcome for prehistoric lithic technologists, as we shall see in later chapters.

Our discussion has set out the basic process that is involved in working through a design theory approach. For prehistorians it really entails finding out everything you can about the basic problems that need to be confronted in living a hunter-gatherer or agricultural lifestyle (or whatever cultural lifestyle your assemblage represents). In this respect experiential and experimental archaeology are invaluable. I listed most of the constraints and design considerations in a chart that may help conceptualize the process for stone tools (Figure 2.1).

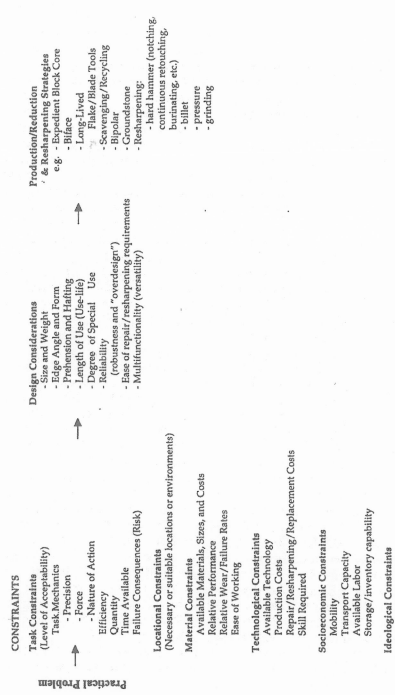

Figure 2.1. This flowchart shows the steps and constraints involved in developing a tool according to design theory as applied to stone tools. (From Hayden 1998, p. 5, Figure 1)

PRESTIGE TECHNOLOGIES

Until now we have been dealing with what I would call practical technologies. Practical technologies are related to the basic needs of life: getting enough food, getting shelter, staying warm, and getting by. Practical technologies adhere to Zipf's Principle of Least Effort. Spending too much time and effort on opening a bottle of beer may mean that you don't get your fire lit or tent put up or food prepared. Thus, in general, you try to do things as efficiently and effectively as possible. Practical technologies seem to have dominated the cultural landscape for the first two and a half million years of human or proto-human existence. There is very little indication of any other considerations in formulating the design of stone tools.

However, when societies became more complex, other considerations also became important—particularly how to influence people, how to create support groups, and how to acquire power. These are the realms of politics and social complexity. New types of problems and technologies emerged with these changes in society: how to indebt others, how to gain access to another family's resources, how to marry into a wealthy family, how to get others to produce surpluses, how to manipulate those surpluses to one's own advantage, how to have claims recognized to ancestral or supernatural powers, and so on.

A variety of material artifacts played key roles in solving the social, political, and ritual problems in these societies. These materials are referred to as prestige items, wealth items, or status items. They consisted of stone, bone, clothing (hides), metals, feathers, plant foods, meats, pets, and an array of other things that could be made into prestige items. They were used to impress others, display one's wealth and one's control over labor, give to others in order to create alliances or indebtedness, certify important events like marriages, and pay for privileges. Chipped, ground, and sculpted stone objects that took on new forms were sometimes developed as part of this prestige menagerie.

With a few exceptions, we will not be dealing with these kinds of stone artifacts. However, from a design perspective it is critical to realize that prestige items require a different approach in order to understand how they differ from practical items. To begin with, the problems to be solved are not practical problems, but sociopolitical problems. Of utmost importance is the fact that the constraints and production processes are turned on their heads. Instead of solving problems in the most efficient way possible to save time and effort, the underwriters of prestige items tried to spend as much effort, time, and resources as possible—and as warranted by the goal—in order to make something that would impress or indebt the intended recipient or spectator to the greatest extent possible.

EXERCISE

In class or at home (groups of three work well), the goal is to make a container to carry four liters (one gallon) of berries. Materials are those *natural* things within thirty minutes walking. What solutions can you come up with? Pick one solution and make the container that you chose. No industrial tools are allowed to be used. What stone tools did you use, if any? Would all solutions involve using stone tools? Try filling your container with nuts or pebbles or berries and carrying it for fifteen minutes to make sure it works effectively. Do you think another solution would be better? Why? How much time did your solution take? How much time do you think other solutions would take? How could you improve on the solution you chose?

ADDITIONAL READINGS

Hayden, Brian. 1998. Practical and Prestige Technologies: The Evolution of Material Systems. *Journal of Archaeological Method and Theory* 5:1–55. This is a major publication promoting the use of design theory to understand both practical and prestige technologies. It delves into details about how design theory has to be structured differently to deal with prestige technologies.

Hayden, Brian, Nora Franco, and Jim Spafford. 1996. Evaluating Lithic Strategies and Design Criteria. In *Stone Tools: Theoretical Insights into Human Prehistory*, edited by George H. Odell, pp. 9–45. Plenum, New York. A significant attempt to apply a design theory analysis to an entire archaeological assemblage of stone tools. It provides the details for the analysis presented in Chapter 8. It also discusses some of the problematic issues in attempts to apply abstract design considerations like versatility, maintainability, reliability, and curation.

Hayden, Brian, and Rob Gargett. 1988. Specialization in the Paleolithic. *Lithic Technology* 17:12–18. This study shows how the quantity of material processed results in increasing investment in making more efficient, and more specialized, tools.

Horsfall, Gayel. 1987. A Design Theory Perspective on Variability in Grinding Stones. In *Lithic Studies Among the Contemporary Highland Maya*, edited by Brian Hayden, pp. 332–378. University of Arizona Press, Tucson. There aren't very many applications of design theory to archaeological assemblages or types of tools. If you want to see what a design theory analysis of a tool type looks like in detail, this is a good example although it doesn't deal with chipped stone.

Kleindienst, Maxine. 1975. Comment. *Current Anthropology* 16:382–383. This is the first published proposal for archaeologists to adopt design theory as a means to understand how artifacts allow people to adapt to their environments in given cultural contexts.

Rousseau, Michael K. 1992. *Integrated Lithic Analysis: The Significance and Function of Key-Shaped Formed Unifaces on the Interior Plateau of Northwestern North America.* Archaeology Press, Simon Fraser University, Burnaby, British Columbia, Canada. Another good example of a design theory analysis of a specific tool type, this time dealing with an unusual scraper type of chipped stone tool.

Sellet, Frédéric. 1993. *Chaîne Opératoire*: The Concept and Its Applications. *Lithic Technology* 18:106–112. While the *chaîne opératoire* approach to analysis may be obscure for many anglophone archaeologists, Sellet explains it clearly and charts a relatively holistic potential use for applying the approach to lithic technologies, which somewhat resembles design theory. However, as it has been used by the French, it is essentially a very descriptive approach of the choices of raw materials and the sequences of actions involved in making, using, and discarding stone tools without much emphasis on explanation.

CHAPTER 3

DESIGN THEORY AS APPLIED
TO LITHIC ANALYSIS

Not all tools are specially designed for specific uses. Some, like utilized flakes, were expedient tools that could have been used to solve a wide range of technological problems—anything from shaving basketry elements (probably women's tasks) to sharpening wooden or bone spear tips, cutting hair or string, or scraping small hides. However, other types clearly were designed with one or possibly two functions in mind. Examples of these are the projectile points, drills, leaf-shaped bifaces, spall scrapers, and end scrapers. It is usually easiest to identify key constraints in the analysis of tools that were specially designed for limited functions—that is, to solve specific problems. So we will look at one of these tool types, end scrapers or the *grattoirs* of the French, from an ethnographic, experiential, and design perspective.

END SCRAPERS: A SPECIALLY DESIGNED TOOL TYPE

End scrapers are one of the most easily identifiable and frequently occurring specialized stone tools. Archaeologists also have a relatively good idea what they were used for: scraping hides. For all these reasons, they constitute a good case study of how design theory can help in the analysis of stone tools. End scrapers often occur on elongated or blade-like flakes (unless resharpened down to a nub, in which case they are referred to as thumbnail scrapers). Their working edge is at the end of the flake—that is, the end opposite the bulb of percussion. The working edge is typically about 2–3 centimeters in width and has a carefully made, very distinctive, regular crescent outline (Figure 3.1). Fine-grained or cryptocrystalline materials are preferred for making them.

Figure 3.1. This ethnographic Arapaho hafted end scraper displays all the classic features of archaeological end scrapers. Photo by Victor Krantz, Catalogue #E200303, courtesy of the Department of Anthropology, National Museum of Natural History, Smithsonian Institution.

Using a design theory approach, it is most useful if we can determine what problem end scrapers were meant to solve. Following this we can look at the most effective edge shapes, types of flakes, methods of core reduction, materials, and other aspects to see how each aspect helped create an optimal design to solve the problem at hand. As we will see, there are a number of alternative ways not only to skin a cat, but to make buckskin as well—not all of which involve end scrapers. To iterate, in using design theory in archaeology, it is not enough just to identify the use of a tool; one must also include consideration of other acceptable design solutions to dealing with problems. For end scrapers used to make buckskin, these could include side scrapers, utilized flakes, broken flakes, truncated flakes, and bone "beamers" or chisels. We then need to determine why end scrapers (rather than other tools) were chosen as the solution.

Moreover, it is not enough to simply state that end scrapers were used to scrape hides. This is far too vague. We need to know at what point in the hide-tanning process end scrapers were used, whether on wet or dry or semi-dry hides, whether for removing hair, epidermis, or membranes, whether for thinning thick hides, and how else these operations could be accomplished using other tool solutions. So understanding end scrapers entails knowing a lot about the process and alternative procedures involved in hide tanning. We need to understand the entire system involved in producing buckskin and all the viable solutions.

To make this point using another example, if we want to know why the Intuit used steatite or ceramic bowls for cooking fish, it would not be enough just to know that the bowls were used to cook fish. We would need to know *why* these bowls were chosen rather than simply roasting the fish over an open flame, cooking the fish in a bark or skin container or a wooden bowl, or simply eating the fish raw. Does cooking really provide any nutritional gain over eating raw or dried fish (fish are often eaten raw or dried)? Were prestige considerations important for special events? How often were fish cooked and in what quantities? How much fuel was available? How much could be cooked in a container? Was oil extraction the goal of cooking? These and other issues are the components of the design system that need to be understood in order to adequately account for the risky adoption of steatite or ceramic bowls in the Arctic—where producing pottery is problematic, transport of heavy items is costly, and ceramics are always vulnerable to breakage among mobile groups.

If end scrapers are important to your lithic analysis, I would highly recommend becoming familiar with a number of "how to" books on making traditional buckskin. Try out both the "dry-scrape" and "wet-scrape" methods yourself using stone tools. There are professional butchers for hunters of game animals in most cities, and it is often possible to get hides from them—or from hunting organizations or even abattoirs.

THE PROBLEM

To begin our analysis of end scrapers, we need to know something more about what problem they were developed to solve. We are unusually fortunate to have a number of very good ethnographic observations on the use of end scrapers to help in the initial formulation of our analysis. John Murdoch recorded the Inuit using hafted end scrapers to prepare animal hides in Alaska. Collections in the Smithsonian Institution also testify to their use on the Great Plains. Sylvie Beyries published some of the most detailed studies from Northern British Columbia and Siberia, while Kathrine Weedman—following Desmond Clark and Hiro Kura-shina and later James Gallagher—documented in considerable detail the hafted use of end scrapers by specialized hideworkers in Ethiopia.

From all these ethnographic observations, it seems fairly well es-tablished that hafted end scrapers were used as a solution for preparing hides, but what aspect of hide preparation? Aside from the Ethiopian end scrapers used by specialists in scraping cow hides, all other ethno-graphic examples were of end scrapers being used for making buckskin or similar soft types of leather. So we will focus on their use in making buckskin, which was the most likely use among prehistoric hunter-gath-erers.

However, making buckskin is a relatively complex process, more so than you might think. In order to understand the specific task end scrap-ers were used for, we need to examine a number of critical steps in mak-ing buckskin that traditionally involved tools—including potential alternatives to end scrapers.

Step 1: Dehairing and Removing the Epidermis

Removing hair and the top layer of ungulate skin (Figure 3.2) are nec-essary to make buckskin—that is, soft leather similar to suede suitable for tailored clothing. This is often done when the hide is wet, usually with a sharpened bone or hard wood "spokeshave," but I have found that end scrapers are also very useful and that right-angled (e.g., broken or truncated) flakes should have been very effective as well. Alterna-tively, the hair and epidermis can be removed when the hide is dry and stretched on a frame. In this case end scrapers are the only really effec-tive traditional tool to use since a sharp tool is required, but one that is not so sharp that it will cut into a hide. When there are numerous kills or time constraints, many hides are simply dried and stored until there is enough time later to work on them—and working hides *is* time con-suming. Hides can always be rehydrated and worked either wet or dry. The thickness of hides is a critical factor as well, since very thick hides require much more thinning, while very thin hides can often tear if scraped with normal end scrapers.

Step 2: Defleshing

Theoretically, removing the remaining flesh from the inside of the skin should not be necessary for ungulates if the skinning is done properly. However, this is often not the case and tools like bone chisels, end scrap-ers, side scrapers, spall tools, or bone spokeshaves could be used when the hide is wet, or end scrapers used when the hide is dry to remove any remaining fat or muscle (Figure 3.3). If flesh is left on the skin, it

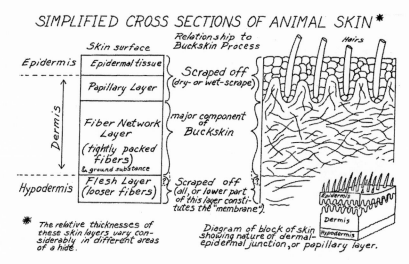

Figure 3.2. A schematic cross-section of skin layers. Note in particular the location of the membrane in the hypodermis. (From Riggs 1980, p. 43)

will become infested and putrify. Handheld side scrapers—rather than hafted scrapers—or chisels were apparently used around the lacing holes at the edges of hides on frames, since more care is necessary to avoid tearing the lacing holes.

Step 3: Removing the Inner Membrane

The lowest layer of skin (the endoderm, just above the flesh and fat on the inside of the hide in all mammals) forms a membrane that will prevent the hide from softening and thus must be removed to make soft leather. This is often done when the hide is wet with the same tools used in Step 2. I have also removed the membrane when dry or almost dry using an end scraper; however, a sharp edge is needed and scraping the membrane quickly dulls the edge. Some experienced hideworkers claim that tools are really only essential to remove this membrane for making soft leather from a properly skinned animal, although a lot more time and effort are needed for the other steps if no other tools are used. If the membrane is not removed, the skin will be like stiff cardboard when it dries.

Step 4: Stretching and Working the Hide

This is necessary to do as the hide dries to prevent fibers in the skin from locking up as they dry. Hides that have locked-up fibers from drying

Figure 3.3. A Nlaka'pamux woman using a hafted spall tool to soften and abrade a large hide. (From Teit 1900, Plate XIV)

without stretching are also stiff like cardboard. There are many ways of stretching hides: from pulling them over rope cables and/or upright stakes, poking them on frames with wooden sticks, pressing into them with spall tools hafted on long (one meter or more) sticks, or simply stretching and rubbing them with the hands.

Step 5: Abrading the Hide

Abrasion is useful to remove any remaining bits of membrane, meat, or fat, and to take off any crusty fibers at the surface. Any rough stone can be used, as well as dry spongy bone or spall scrapers (as in Step 4).

Design Lessons from Making Buckskin

There are five important lessons to be learned from this little ethnographic foray.

(1) It should be evident that there are usually multiple technological solutions to almost everything. Jim Riggs captured this nicely in ob-

serving that everyone who makes buckskin today does things slightly differently, but they all work. It should also be remembered that buckskin was probably not the only option or solution for clothing in many areas. Even in the British Columbia plateau where winter temperatures regularly reach 30–40 degrees below zero, poor individuals often used shredded bark for clothes or had no substantial clothes at all.

(2) End scrapers do not exist in isolation. They are part of a larger set of tools used to produce soft leather, often including bone chisels or beamers, stone or bone abraders (either unmodified cobbles or hafted spall tools), side scrapers, possibly flakes with right-angled edges, and various tools (including hafted spall scrapers) used to stretch the hides as they dry.

(3) Even where stone tools were used, as in softening or abrading leather, there can be alternatives using organic materials like wood or rope that would leave no archaeological traces.

(4) End scrapers are specific to scraping hides, usually for the removal of one or more layers of a hide.

(5) It is interesting to note that, except for Ethiopia where hideworking is a specialized craft in which men also work, all the accounts of hunter-gatherers feature women as the sole hideworkers. End scrapers, as well as spall tools, abrading stones, bone chisels, and beamers, are therefore probably gender indicators of tasks. Buckskin clothing was also very time consuming to make and demanded a lot of effort. It was therefore costly and in many groups was considered a great investment and an important sign of wealth. In these cases end scrapers could also be seen as indicators of the manufacturing of major prestige items that were produced for display and exchange (Figure 3.4). Stone tools do not often imply gender, social, prestige, or unusual economic values, but end scrapers are one of the important cases where they do.

In sum, in interpreting the prehistoric activities that occurred at a site, we need to take a broad perspective and consider tools related to a given task and other possible materials used in those tasks.

DECONSTRUCTING END SCRAPERS: THE DESIGN FACTORS

We have reviewed the major task constraints for making soft leather or buckskin for clothes. The essential problems are removing the epidermis (hair and outer skin—that is, the "grain") and the endodermis (the inside membrane), as well as any adhering meat and fat on the underside. To remove these layers, hides can be worked either wet with bone tools or dry with stone tools. There are advantages and disadvantages to both

Figure 3.4. Traditional buckskin clothes of two high-ranking Nlaka'pamux members. Such clothes were major wealth items, and even today new versions of clothes like this would cost many thousands of dollars. *Left.* Nlaka'pamux (Thompson) woman wearing traditional buckskin clothing, Spences Bridge, British Columbia. James Teit, 1913. Canadian Museum of History, #23212. *Right.* Nlaka'pamux (Thompson) Chief John Tetlenitsa in traditional clothing and holding a war club, Ottawa, Ontario. Edward Sapir, 1916. Canadian Museum of History, #35995.

that we won't go into here. We are mainly interested in the constraints for scraping dry hides.

Material Constraints

First of all, for effectively removing either the dry epidermis or the membrane from ungulate hides, a sharp and resharpenable type of stone is needed—one that can be shaped to fit into a haft for greatest efficiency if sizable skins and/or many skins are to be worked. This means using a relatively high-quality cryptocrystalline or non-crystalline material with a conchoidal fracture like chert, flint, chalcedony, vitrified tuffs, vitreous rhyolites or mafic rocks, or obsidian. If none of these are easily available, special efforts must be made to obtain them, or alternative strategies (e.g., shifting to wet scraping with bone tools) must be used.

Task Constraints

The cutting edge of the tool needs to be sharp to be effective but not so sharp that it will easily cut through the hide or create gouges in it. This means that edge angles can't be too low and there can be no projections creating a jagged cutting edge. Edges of flakes just removed from cores are too sharp and must be dulled with retouch, and the retouch must be continuous and uniform. Furthermore, if the skins are worked stretched in a frame (as were most native North American and Siberian skins), then straight or concave edges would be much less effective than convex edges. Straight or concave edges would exert too much pressure at their angled ends and risk puncturing the hides. The same design logic can be seen in modern metal defleshing tools (Figure 3.5).

Size and Kinematic Constraints

To most successfully remove layers of skin, small strips only 1–3 centimeters wide need to be removed. Thus the working edge should be about the same size.

While handheld tools can be effectively used to remove layers of skin, this becomes difficult to continue for long periods and scraping a single deer hide usually takes from one to four hours of strong pressure

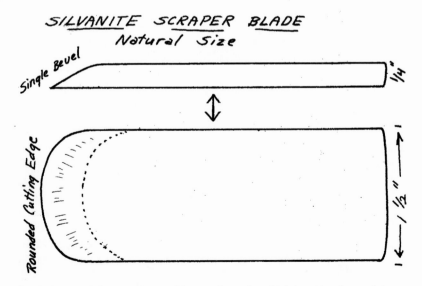

Figure 3.5. Metal scrapers used by modern deer hide tanners have the same form as traditional stone end scrapers. (From Riggs 1980, p. 40)

scraping. Thus working with hafted stone scrapers becomes highly advantageous. It allows more pressure to be exerted with the tool and the tool to be grasped in a more comfortable manner, even using two hands.

Skill Constraints

The production of scraper blanks that can be sharpened many times may entail specialized expertise in knapping—for instance, in the production of blades for end scrapers. However, less stringent demands for resharpening and material conservation could be met by simple elongated flakes that many people would have been able to produce. Once the flakes are made, the retouching (resharpening) of the blanks is a skill that most individuals should have been capable of mastering.

Technological Constraints

While the membrane may be more efficiently removed from wet hides using a bone beamer, in many assemblages—such as the Upper Paleolithic ones in Europe and the ethnographic examples in Ethiopia—there are no archaeological bone tools present that would have been suitable for removing skin layers in this fashion. In these cases it can tentatively be assumed that all layers of skin were removed using stone scraping tools.

Quantity

The amount of area that requires scraping also affects tool design. The size and number of hides will affect the number of resharpenings and/or the number of tools required. Scraping just one deer hide involves working a surface with an area of 1–2 square meters. Removing the membrane or hair/epidermis with any dirt adhering can be highly abrasive, requiring resharpening or replacing the scraping tool every 5–10 minutes. In effect, ethnographic accounts of end scraper use by the Inuit reported resharpening end scrapers every few minutes. Resharpening—rather than replacing—tools is by far the most efficient option. Thus tools need to be designed for repeated resharpenings if material conservation is any consideration, which it usually is given transport constraints (limited transport capacities) and high procurement costs of suitable stone material from long distances.

Size Matters

An important thing to keep in mind is that fur-bearing animals like foxes, lynx, skunks, raccoons, and rabbits have much thinner skins, much thinner membranes, and much more fat. The hair is the main purpose for processing these hides, so it is frequently left on. Once the fat and membrane are removed with a scraper (either handheld or hafted), the skins are softened simply by rubbing and abrading and can even be used without tanning. Sometimes the membrane doesn't even need to be removed.

Skins of small animals like squirrels and ermine were also sometimes used to trim buckskin clothes. The skins were dried and then simply abraded with a coarse-grained pebble or cobble to help soften them and remove remaining fat or flesh. Interestingly, the skins of the marsupial animals in Australia have much thinner membranes than similar-sized mammals and thus usually do not require the removal of the membrane using stone tools. As a result, there are no end scraper hide-working stone tools in Australian assemblages.

DESIGNING HIDE–SCRAPING TOOLS

Overall the design characteristics of hideworking tools can be affected by a number of considerations or constraints. At a minimum these include:

- Thickness of the skin.
- Area of the skin.
- Number of skins to be processed.
- Presence or absence of an internal membrane.
- Amount of fat and meat requiring removal.
- Hair density and cleanliness.
- Retaining the fur or not.
- Dry versus wet removal of the hair and epidermis.
- Availability of suitable lithic materials.

A range of differently designed hideworking tools were undoubtedly used since these factors varied. But for making buckskin from dry stretched ungulate hides, taking all these constraints into consideration yields the recurring optimal solution for removing the required layers of skin from hides: a high-grade stone material that could be shaped into a very uniform convex working edge 2–3 centimeters wide, capable of being resharpened multiple times. Edge angles would initially have been 60–70 degrees but could become more abrupt as the tool approached the last possible resharpenings. This essentially is a description of an end scraper.

The ethnographic examples discussed above had several important characteristics in common.

- Their working edge was almost always the distal end of a somewhat elongated or oval flake capable of being resharpened multiple times.
- The working edge was always very regular and convex without any points sticking out along the edge.
- Most working edges were about 1–3 centimeters in width.
- The edge angles of end scrapers ranged from 55 degrees to over 90 degrees (averaging 75 degrees).
- Fine-grained cryptocrystalline rocks or non-crystalline rocks like obsidian were strongly favored as raw materials.

These combinations of design features are not duplicated for any other hunter-gatherer task that I know of. There may be one-off chance similarities of individual tools like the "end scraper" that was reportedly used to scrape out the inside of a wild yam in Central Australia, or elongated flakes with blunted ends for prehension (also in Australia), but this is not the same kind of situation as a standardized tool type that occurs repeatedly in regional assemblages. Thus, when lithic analysts find end scrapers in assemblages (especially if there are a lot of them, as in the European Upper Paleolithic or on the North American Great Plains), we can be fairly confident that these were tools designed for making soft leather clothing.

The use-wear from scraping hides is also quite distinctive. Although some analysts have found other use-wear traces on end scrapers, this should not be taken to mean that end scrapers were designed for other uses. All it means is that end scrapers were the most convenient tool at hand when something was needed for another purpose.

BLADES AND REDUCTION STRATEGIES

It may be evident at this point that one of the best resharpenable designs for end scrapers used for large hides or large quantities of hides is to make them on blades. Blades can be repeatedly resharpened like pencils—right down to the nubs in the hafts where they can't be sharpened or easily used anymore.

However, the issue of why formal, standardized blades developed in some regions and during some prehistoric periods and not others has perplexed prehistorians for many years, and there have been a number of suggestions to account for the creation and maintenance of the highly skilled flint-knapping abilities required for the systematic production of blades. We will return to this topic in Chapter 5, but it can be noted for now that high mobility and the need to conserve raw (lithic) material have been invoked to account for these developments. Few people have thought about design constraints like high volumes of processing materials, whether of hides or meat. This is particularly pertinent for the European Upper Paleolithic and the North American Paleoindian periods.

While the occasional making of buckskin in many areas could be carried out with the production of somewhat elongated flakes from block cores, higher volumes of processing would have placed considerably more pressure on individuals to find ways of extending the use-lives or the number of resharpenings of hide scrapers. In the interior of British Columbia, modern hunter-gatherers living in houses needed to process about one hide per person per year; and if stone scrapers were used, elongated flakes that could be produced from simple block cores would probably be adequate. However, if the requirements for working hides were significantly greater due either to working heavier hides or processing more hides for exchange, clothing, or shelter, then core reduction techniques favoring longer flakes (i.e., blades) that could be resharpened a greater number of times should have been favored.

But there is another design-related reason why blade production may have been important prehistorically, and it is also related to high processing volumes—namely, the fine filleting of large amounts of meat for drying and preserving as jerky. In order to cut meat into thin strips for drying, a long, straight cutting edge is most effective and efficient. A simple primary flake with a sharp edge can certainly perform this task, but it would be relatively slow, would produce irregular cuts, and would be awkward to use. It would be like trying to cut roast beef or turkey into thin slices with a very small pocketknife rather than a carving knife. As long as the amounts to be filleted are small, as with an occasional small deer or goat, simple primary flakes (utilized flakes) would be adequate—even if a little messy. The extra time and effort required to develop the expertise to fashion proper cores in order to make more efficient blades would be entirely out of proportion to the small benefit obtained to fillet a small animal.

However, when large amounts of meat need to be processed in short periods of time (as with butchering mass kills of dozens or scores of animals like caribou/reindeer or even single large game animals like bison, mammoths, bears, or rhinoceros), then something far more efficient is required in order to dry the meat and prevent the loss of large portions of the kill before spoilage. Aside from large metal knives, blades provide one of the most optimal solutions under these constraints.

A terminological note of caution is warranted here. In some areas of North America, the term "blades" refers to bifaces. While it is true that most bifaces are more than twice as long as they are wide, they are technologically very different from what most prehistorians refer to as blades (see Chapter 5).

DISCUSSION

While we have benefited from ethnographic observations on the basic use of end scrapers and can understand the distinctive end scraper characteristics from a design perspective, what do we do when confronted with stone tool types that we have no ethnographic information about? Handaxes, notches, burins, expedient knives, truncated flakes or blades, and other types constitute problematic cases in this regard.

The best approach is to carefully examine context, use-wear, residues, and the closest similar types with known uses, and to use the design theory approach—working backward from observed characteristics of the tool to a problem that makes sense in terms of those characteristics. What kind of lithic material was used and how available was it? How sharp could the edges be? How brittle or tough was the material? How many resharpenings were used? What type of retouch was used? What shape were the edges? How big was it? Was it hafted? What was the edge angle? How can these and other features be used to reconstruct a reasonable task for which the type was used? In order to address some of these issues, we need to know what basic modifications could be and were made to the naturally occurring flake edges, what their identifying characteristics were, and whether there is any ethnographic information about how different types of modified edges were used. This is the topic of the next chapter.

EXERCISE

Design a stone tool that is capable of felling one tree that is ten centimeters in diameter. Identify all the constraints and design features. Propose an alternative solution (using stone or other materials).

How would your design change if you had to fell a hundred trees fifteen centimeters in diameter (e.g., to build a pithouse) or one tree one meter in diameter (e.g., for a dugout canoe)?

ADDITIONAL READINGS

End Scraper Ethnographies

Albright, Sylvia L. 1984. *Tahltan Ethnoarchaeology*. Publication No. 15, Archaeology Department, Simon Fraser University, Burnaby, British Columbia, Canada. Although Albright does not deal with end scrapers, she does document the traditional techniques for producing buckskin, including the use of stone spall scrapers/abraders. This is a key resource for researchers who have spall scrapers in their assemblages. Albright is one of the very few archaeologists who has studied the use of these scrapers among hunting-gathering groups and documented in detail the procedures for making buckskin.

Beyries, Sylvie. 2008. Modélisation du travail du cuir en ethnologie. *Anthropozoologica* 48:9–42. Beyries is also one of the very few archaeologists who has studied chipped stone manufacturing and use among hunter-gatherers. She specifically went to northern British Columbia and Siberia in order to study the processing of ungulate hides with stone and bone scrapers, including end scrapers and their use-wear. Although this article is in French, it is a key resource.

Clark, J. Desmond, and Hiro Kurashina. 1981. A Study of the Work of a Modern Tanner in Ethiopia and Its Relevance for Archaeological Interpretation. In *Modern Material Culture: The Archaeology of Us*, edited by Richard A. Gould and Michael B. Schiffer, pp. 303–321. Academic Press, New York. One of the first articles to signal that stone tools were still being used by some agricultural groups in Ethiopia to scrape hides.

Gallagher, James P. 1977. Contemporary Stone Tools in Ethiopia: Implications for Archaeology. *Journal of Field Archaeology* 4:407–414. Gallagher followed up on Clark and Kurashina's report with much more detailed observations and illustrations of the end scrapers used by specialist hideworkers to produce cow hides for making beds.

Hayden, Brian. 1979. Snap, Shatter, and Superfractures: Use-Wear of Stone Skin Scrapers. In *Lithic Use-Wear Analysis*, edited by Brian Hayden, pp. 207–230. Academic Press, New York. This article presents an analysis of Inuit hafted end scrapers collected in the late nineteenth century in Alaska and now housed in the Smithsonian Institution. It documents their use and their use-wear.

Hayden, Brian. 1990. The Right Rub: Hide Working in High Ranking Households. In *The Interpretative Possibilities of Microwear Studies: Proceedings of the International Conference on Lithic Use-Wear Analysis, 15th–17th February 1989 in Uppsala, Sweden (Aun)*, edited by Bo Graslund, pp. 89–102. Societas Archaeologica Upsaliensis, Uppsala. From previous work it was evident that buckskin clothes were very costly in terms of the time, effort, and skill needed to produce buckskin. They were prestige items and the frequency of stone tools like end scrapers might therefore be indicators of differential wealth between hearth groups or households.

Murdoch, John. 1892. *Ethnological Results of the Point Barrow Expedition.* Ninth Annual Report of the Bureau of American Ethnology, Government Printing Office, Washington, DC. This tome is one of the classic ethnographies of the late nineteenth century. It is especially valuable for the collections of traditional material culture, the photographs of items, and the description of their uses—including hafted end scrapers used in working hides.

Wedel, Waldo R. 1970. Antler Tine Scraper Handles in the Central Plains. *Plains Anthropologist* 15:36–45. The Great Plains Indians were also very active in working buffalo hides into buckskin and making prestigious clothes with buckskin. There are few hafted ethnographic specimens with chipped stone bits, but Wedel mentions several and illustrates how scrapers were hafted. I could only locate one example in the Smithsonian of a Plains haft with a stone end scraper.

Weedman, Kathryn J. 2006. An Ethnoarchaeological Study of Hafting and Stone Tool Diversity Among the Gamo of Ethiopia. *Journal of Archaeological Method and Theory* 13:189–237. Weedman is the latest archaeologist to study the hide scrapers used in Ethiopia. While previous ethnoarchaeologists provided good documentation on a few specialists and their tools, Weedman documents the variability in end scraper (or other) tool morphologies and materials over a wide region and attempts to explain why tools had different morphologies.

Experiments and Analysis in Hideworking

Edholm, Steven, and Tamara Wilder. 1997. *Wet-Scrape Braintanned Buckskin: A Practical Guide to Home Tanning and Use.* Paleotechnics, Boonville, California. There are two basic approaches to working ungulate hides in order to remove the epiderm: wet scrape and dry scrape. There are disadvantages and advantages to both, as well as advocates for both techniques. This book tells you everything you need to know about the wet-scrape technique.

Kamminga, Johan. 1982. *Over the Edge: Functional Analysis of Australian Stone Tools.* Occasional Papers in Anthropology No. 12, Anthropology Museum, University of Queensland, Brisbane, Australia. Probably the most comprehensive experimental study of Australian lithic tools and use-wear, this is a very valuable resource documenting the ethnographic use of stone tools by Australian Aborigines.

Riggs, Jim. 1980. *Blue Mountain Buckskin: A Working Manual – Dry-Scrape Brain-Tan.* Self-published, Wallowa, Oregon. Riggs is one of the foremost proponents of using dry scrape techniques to produce buckskin.

He clearly sets out the advantages and disadvantages of dry- versus wet-scrape techniques. For dry scrape removal of the epidermis, end scrapers appear to be the optimal tool. Even the metal scraping tools he uses look like end scrapers.

Stone Bowls and Ceramics

Hayden, Brian. 2019. Use of Ceramic Technologies by Circumpolar Hunter-Gatherers. In *Ceramics in Circumpolar Prehistory: Technology, Lifeways and Cuisine*, edited by Peter Jordon and Kevin Gibbs, pp. 216–226. Cambridge University Press, Cambridge, UK. Although the focus of this commentary is on why ceramics were adopted in poorly suited environments like the Arctic, it exemplifies the kind of questions and issues that design theory raises in understanding tool solutions to practical and prestige problems.

CHAPTER 4

TIER 1:
ANALYZING STONE TOOLS

There is something basic that you need to know before starting to an-alyze stone tools. Notably, a great deal of traditional tool use is ex-temporaneous and expedient.

EXPEDIENT, EXTEMPORANEOUS,
AND OPPORTUNISTIC TOOL USE

Before getting into the nuts and bolts, or tools and debitage, of stone tools, I would like to emphasize one of the major lessons that I learned in Australia—that is, the expedient way in which many tools are used. If one type of rock is not available, another less suitable and less effec-tive stone (often non-cryptocrystalline) will generally be enlisted to do the job, sometimes even one with a naturally angled edge that is never retouched or modified in any way (Figure 4.1). Tools could just be nat-ural pieces of ordinary stone, whether for carving out wooden bowls or snapping the ribs off a kangaroo in butchering. Hunting-gathering life is often situational. When a task occurs that needs to be done, you look around to see if there is a good tool at hand. If not, you look around to see what else might work. Sometimes you have to be creative and make do with solutions that barely work.

As emphasized in the last chapter, this point becomes important when some lithic analysts conclude that specially designed types of tools (like end scrapers) were not made for hide scraping, because the use-wear on their ends shows they were used on wood and bone as well as on hides. In industrial cultures flathead screwdrivers were clearly de-signed for only one purpose. However, look at the use-wear of old screwdrivers that might soon be ready to be tossed out. It should be

Figure 4.1. An Aboriginal Australian woman using a naturally occurring block of stone for thinning down the back of a wooden bowl at Cundeelee, Western Australia.

fairly easy to tell that these old pieces have been used in the garden for digging out weeds, for prying open paint cans, for removing old paint from tight crevasses, and a host of unidentified uses that have worn down the edges of the screwdriver. This does not mean that screwdrivers weren't designed for dealing with screws.

I am convinced that paleo people, like modern hunter-gatherers and household handymen, used whatever was at hand when they needed a tool for a particular task. In most cases (there are some exceptions), if a specially designed tool was not immediately available, they just used whatever piece of stone was at hand, even if it didn't work as well as a tool especially made for the job. Thus I feel fairly certain that end scrapers were designed and made for one thing only: working hides, no matter what use-wear may be present.

Design theory is particularly good for reconstructing the function and constraints of specially designed tools like end scrapers. It is also useful for understanding the development of much less specialized tools with a variety of potential uses, although in these cases it may not be possible to identify the specific function from a design perspective, or even to determine that an object was actually used as a tool—as in the case of an unmodified rock picked up for expedient use as a convenient tool (whether used as a hammerstone, tent weight, chopper, grinder, or for other useful functions). In both cases—specialized tools and tools that could function in a number of potentially different ways—design theory helps explain the different strategies adopted to knap tool blanks from cores, a topic that will be addressed in the next chapter.

THE NUTS AND BOLTS OF ANALYZING STONE TOOLS: TOOLS AND DEBITAGE

In order to determine how stone tools were used to solve problems, we have to know what can be done with stones, how they can be modified to be suitable for various tasks, how fast they dull during use in different tasks and then need to be resharpened or replaced, their availability or replacement costs, skill levels required to make some tools, and a number of other factors. The purpose of this chapter is to describe how we can determine that a cryptocrystalline or vitreous stone has been modified by people and how such stones can be more specifically modified to make them suitable for various tasks. The main advantage of cryptocrystalline and non-crystalline stones is that they can be used to create sharp cutting edges that can be resharpened if needed.

An Artifact or Not an Artifact?

When you pick up a flake, the first thing is to determine whether it is a natural stone or something made by a person. With cryptocrystalline or vitreous materials, the key indicators are usually found on the ventral side (the side that was inside the core). These indicators consist of (a) the presence of a bulb of percussion or point of impact; (b) undulations or ripples that extend out from the point of impact, like ripples when a stone is thrown into water; and (c) fissure lines that radiate out from the point of impact, like rays from the sun or spokes of a wheel radiating out from the hub (Figure 4.2).

In granular materials such as quartzite or impure flints, these features are much harder to see; they may be faint or may not even be present. The occurrence of flake scars on the dorsal side (or outside) of the flake is also a good indicator of an object being manmade, but they are not always present—particularly on the first flakes removed from a nodule. The point of impact, undulations, and radiating fissures are also the first features to look for in orienting the flake and figuring out how it was produced, as well as whether anything was done to it subsequently to make it into a tool. A word of caution: this is a simplified version of a

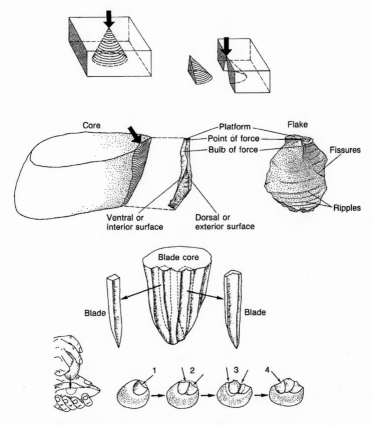

Figure 4.2. Features of flakes and cone-type fractures. A pyramidal blade core and reduction of a cobble either for flakes or for use as a chopper are depicted below. The blade removal on the right side of the core is atypical. (From Hayden 1993, p. 48, Figure 2.5)

complex situation that sometimes becomes very contentious—especially involving very early, questionable industries, for which there is a fairly extensive and detailed literature.

Point of Impact

Flakes often break up when being struck from a core so that the point of impact is frequently missing. Bulbs of percussion can also be intentionally removed either by thinning the bulbar area or by intentionally breaking off the bulb. Thus the first thing to determine is whether the point of impact is present. If not, where would it have been? This can be determined by projecting the undulations and fissures back to an approximate point of origin. Then you need to figure out if the bulb might have been removed intentionally. Is there a point of impact on the broken edge of a flake that would indicate a hammerstone was used to break off the missing part of the flake? Are there any ventral flake removals from the inferred area of impact? If you are unsure what any of these features might look like, try experimenting with thick bottle glass, thick ceramic materials, or actual cryptocrystalline stones if they are available.

It is also important to determine where the point of impact was because part of the striking platform that was originally part of the edge of the core is usually present. Thin edges of cores usually produce short or failed flake removals so that the edges of cores forming striking platforms were frequently modified in order to increase the core edge angle by removing a series of small flakes (Figure 4.3). This very common procedure leaves a series of flake scars along the striking platform edge that look like scraper retouch. A flake removed from a core with a modified edge will carry those modifications along the edge of the striking plat-

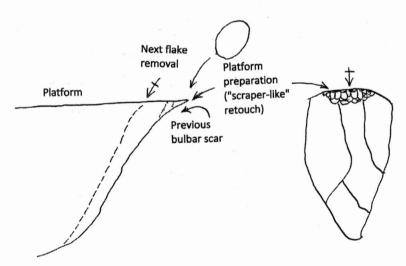

Figure 4.3. Platform preparation retouch is used to strengthen the edges of cores so that flake detachments run farther and produce large versus small flakes. This kind of retouch superficially resembles scraper-resharpening retouch but always originates from the edge of platform remnants, which is why it is so important to identify the points of percussion on flakes.

form remnant of the flake. These "retouches" are located along the edge adjacent to the point of impact. As such, these small flake removals on the striking platform remnant can easily be misidentified as tool modifications, but they are not. They are simply core preparations. Thus it is critically important to know where the point of impact is or was on a flake.

To iterate, the location of the point of impact is the first thing to determine whether the actual point of impact is present or missing. It may be wondered if the edges of the "platform remnants" on flakes were ever used as tools. No. The proximal end of flakes adjoining the point of impact were rarely, if ever, used as tools. Use of platform remnants may not be impossible, but you need very compelling reasons to argue for this kind of use. I have never seen a convincing example.

Debitage versus Primary Flakes

Once you have determined whether or not a flake is whole and where the point of impact is or was, the next step is to find out whether anything has been done to the flake to make it suitable for tool use. However, we also need to recognize that many flakes that have not been intentionally modified may have been used as tools. As many of my mentors liked to point out, the sharpest edge of a flake is the edge that occurs when the flake comes off the core. No amount of retouch will increase the sharpness of a flake unless it has an unusually high edge angle that can be lowered by extensive thinning of the flake. Thus many flakes without any modification may have been used as tools. Peter White and I have abundantly documented this ethnographically. It is also important to realize that the lower the edge angle for any given material, the sharper the edge will be, but it also becomes more fragile and easily broken—especially by trampling.

Following the French usage in François Bordes's lab, I refer to flakes suitable for use as tools as primary flakes. They have at least one good length of cutting edge and are usually large enough to hold in the hand easily. Flakes without any suitable cutting edges due to irregularities in the edge, high edge angles, or dorsal cortex, I refer to as secondary flakes. For whatever reason edges with cortex covering all or most of the dorsal face seem to have been rarely or never used as tools.

Despite the fact that many unmodified flakes may have been used as tools (e.g., see Figure 4.12 below), the only way we can be certain that a flake was used as a tool—aside from use-wear analysis—is to determine if it has been modified (there are a few rare exceptions like Mousterian naturally backed knives). Thus tools are, by traditional definition, modified flakes. Flakes that have not been modified are treated as debitage or waste products. Debitage comes in all sizes. When flakes are being removed from a core, there are usually only a few large flakes, a good number of small pieces of debitage, and a geometrically increasing number of tiny flakes according to size category. There are many ways of analyzing debitage that can be very useful for determining the basic type of core reduction. This will be discussed briefly in Chapter 5.

FLAKE TOOLS: THE SIX SIDES OF A FLAKE

In order to determine whether a flake is a piece of debitage or a tool, you need to carefully inspect the entire flake to see whether there have been any intentional modifications to the flake. The platform remnant and point of impact (or closest side to that end if the flake is broken) constitute the proximal end of a flake. We have already dealt with this side. You need to carefully examine the other five sides to determine whether there have been any modifications. These consist of the distal end (opposite the point of impact), the two sides of the flake, the ventral face, and the dorsal face.

Many flakes have fairly regular edge outlines when they are re-moved from the core. Thus the next thing is to examine the ventral face of a flake. This does two things: first, it should reveal any retouch on the ventral face (which is referred to as inverse retouch); and second, it can immediately alert you to any unusual edge features like notches, buri-nations, or nice convex, concave, or straight edges that may indicate in-tentional modification on the dorsal face of the flake. Lookalike edge outlines similar to these features can be produced by the natural dorsal topography of the flake depending on the configuration of the core, but most often a distinctive edge outline is a good sign of intentional mod-ification on the dorsal face.

Thus the next step is to turn the flake over and closely examine the dorsal face and edges—the distal edge and the two lateral edges—for any signs of edge modification (which is generally referred to as nor-mal retouch). Usually, the vast majority of retouched tools are normally retouched and only occasional tools are inversely or even bifacially re-touched along the edges. This is probably because the dorsal face is usually irregular from previous flake removals, so if this is the face con-tacting the material being worked, it will be irregular and create gouges in the material rather than a smooth cut or scrape, and it will be less ef-ficient. The ventral surface of most flakes is somewhat curved and con-cave; the edge is concave when used normally but convex if used inversely. The concave curve is usually better suited to shaving or scrap-ing cylindrical materials like wood shafts, bone, or antler. If this seems difficult to understand, try using some flakes to shave down a stick nor-mally and inversely. See how they both perform. Why some tools are retouched inversely or bifacially is something of a puzzle, but it is not normal.

Types of Edge Modification

There are two basic things that you want to find out about flake tools: how they have been modified and how they were produced. In this chapter we deal with how they have been modified, and in the next we will discuss how they were produced.

There are eight common basic types of edge modification that can be recognized in most large assemblages—scraper retouch, abrupt retouch, invasive retouch, notches and denticulates or serrations, burinations, battering, bifacial rotary retouch, and intentional breaks. You should become familiar with them. None of these modifications requires great skill and all could have been employed by almost every adult or adolescent in any community.

Scraper Retouch

Scraper retouch is usually defined as semi-abrupt retouch with edge angles ranging from about 55 degrees to 75 degrees. It is made by holding a flake ventral side up and striking a small pebble along one or more ventral edge(s) to remove a series of continuous small flakes from the dorsal face. This creates the ubiquitous "scraper" type that appears in the vast majority of assemblages of the world (Figure 4.4). Scrapers can be classified by their edge shape (straight, convex, concave), degree of retouch (number of resharpenings), orientation (side, transversal, end, double, convergent), or other criteria depending on the purpose of creating or using a given typology (see Chapter 8).

One word of warning: as Norman Tindale and then Harold Dibble demonstrated, extensively resharpened scrapers can go through a number of shape and working edge transformations—starting off as lightly retouched scrapers scarcely different from utilized flakes to flake stubs with stacked step fractures (Figure 4.5). The edge shape might be loosely associated with the degree of retouch, but the meaning (if any) of different shapes and orientations needs to be worked out for each lithic tradition if you want to use those criteria for analyzing scrapers. In all cases scraper retouch is one of the most versatile types of edge modification. It can be used to scrape hides; shave wood, bone, antler, or basket elements; or cut meat, tendons, or fish flesh. Scrapers can be hafted or used handheld. If hafted, the bulb is frequently removed or thinned.

A special type of what may be considered scraper retouch is "Quina retouch," named by the French after the site where it was first recognized. What distinguishes Quina retouch is the prevalence of step fractures in intensively retouched edges. This kind of retouch has been documented by Tindale on hafted flake adzes used in Australia (Figure 4.5*r,s.*), where resharpening was performed with a hard wood percussor like the blade of a boomerang or other piece of wood that is suitably

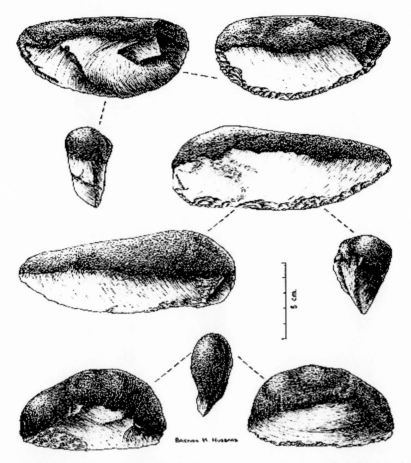

Figure 4.4. Typical scraper (semi-abrupt) retouch on flakes used by Aboriginal Australians for a variety of tasks including as knives, adzes, scrapers, and engravers. The proximal ends have been covered in plant resin for easier use. (From Tindale 1965, p. 142, Figures 6–8; courtesy of the South Australian Museum)

hard and heavy (Figure 4.6). While a hard percussor could remove more material from the flake and rejuvenate the cutting edge, using a pebble is more likely to break the resin hafting so that a softer percussor is employed, even if this results in step fractures and overhangs that eventually make the adze "unresharpenable" and unusable—at which point it is discarded. If scrapers retouched in this way are reversed in the haft so as to use the opposite edge, the resulting exhausted scraper develops into an elongated domed piece with steep step fractures on the sides (Figure 4.5s.) that the French aptly named *limaces*, or "slugs."

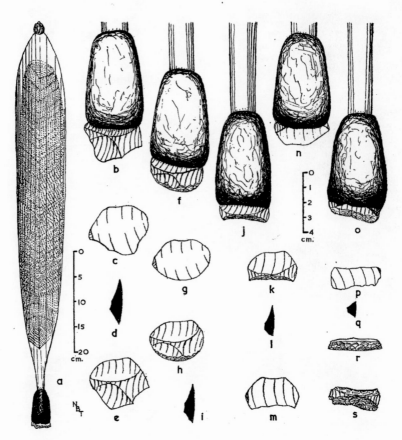

Figure 4.5. Flake adzes hafted onto the end of trough spearthrowers (at left) undergo a number of morphological transformations with successive resharpenings, as diagramatically illustrated here by Norman Tindale. Note the scraper type of retouch in *h* and the extreme abrupt step fracturing in the exhausted stage portrayed in *r* and *s*. (From Tindale 1965, p. 153, Figure 19; courtesy of the South Australian Museum).

Abrupt Retouch

Abrupt retouch is retouch approaching 90 degrees. It typically occurs on types referred to as truncations and backed pieces. Abrupt retouch can be created either by holding a flake in your hand and retouching it with a pebble used at a very oblique striking angle (Figure 4.7), or in the case of backing by placing the flake on a stone anvil and striking the edge carefully with a pebble until a right-angled edge is formed (Fig-

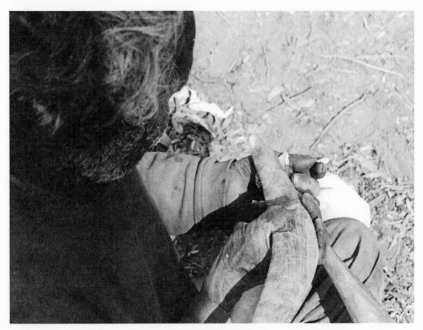

Figure 4.6. Resharpening Australian flake adzes is often done with soft percussors like this hard wood boomerang being used to resharpen an adze hafted onto the end of a spearthrower.

ure 4.8). A number of prehistoric traditions employ backing in order to blunt an edge that might cut one's hand when being used (Figure 4.9 left) or to haft the flake in a more stable fashion using resin—that is, by removing enough of a lateral edge to create a wedge-shaped section similar to the shape that dentists use for fillings. Such tools are often components in composite hafted tools like sickles, knives, or projectiles with blades hafted along their sides.

Truncated flakes, on the other hand, are more problematic. They typically have the distal end abruptly retouched either straight across or on a diagonal (Figure 4.7). One possibility is that they could have been used in removing the epidermis and hair or membrane from wet-scraped hides, since modern tanners like Jim Riggs note that right angles on tools are very effective in these tasks.

Invasive Retouch

Invasive retouch usually has an edge angle of less than 55 degrees and the flake scars usually travel farther across the face of the flake than an

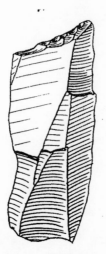

Figure 4.7. An example of a Middle Paleolithic truncated flake probably made with oblique direct percussion. (From Bordes 1961, Plate 38:10)

Figure 4.8. An Aboriginal Australian at Papunya (Northern Territory) removing unwanted parts of a flake so that it can be hafted onto the end of a spearthrower. The flake is placed on an anvil and struck with a hammerstone, exactly as is done to create backing on flakes.

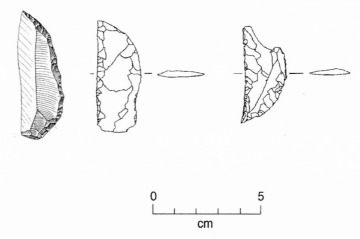

Figure 4.9. *Left.* Example of a backed Mousterian knife (from Bordes 1961, Plate 35:19). *Right.* Examples of expedient knives with invasive retouch from Keatley Creek (from Hayden and Spafford 2000, p. 45, Figure 22; drawing by Suzanne Villeneuve).

equivalent retouch made with a pebble flaker. The invasive flakes on minimally retouched tools are often only a millimeter or two in length, but can be substantially longer on more heavily retouched tools.

On the Canadian Plateaux, billet flakes with very low edge angles (see Chapter 5) were often chosen to make types that I call expedient knives. These are created by using an antler, bone, or hard wood flaker or baton to remove flakes along the working edge via pressure flaking. The side of the flaker or baton is simply pressed into the flake edge and rolled or dragged along the length of the edge that is to be resharpened. The first resharpening can be so small that the flake removals resemble utilized flakes, but this can be repeated a number of times with flakes becoming longer each time.

The original low edge angles of billet flakes, the use of pressure flaking to resharpen dull edges and maintain low angles, and the highly uniform, continuous series of removals all indicate that these were cutting tools for hides or leather or possibly meat (Figure 4.9 right). Many North American archaeologists do not differentiate these kinds of pressure-resharpened flakes from scraper retouch and simply classify them as scrapers. However, the difference is important. Expedient knives were made for very specific tasks, whereas scrapers were much more multi-functional.

Notches, Denticulates, and Serrations

Notches were one of the most puzzling types of retouch that I encountered while studying Mousterian assemblages at the University of Bordeaux. I wondered for years what they could have been used for. They are also one of the most neglected or unrecognized artifact types in North America. If you simply hold a flake with the ventral side up and strike the edge with a pebble to remove a 1–2 centimeter flake from the edge, you have made a notch (Figure 4.10). To accurately identify notches as intentional modifications, they need to display points of impact in order to differentiate them from lookalikes created by dips along the edge of the dorsal surface of the flake, or by the trampling of flakes with thin edges.

When I went to Australia to conduct an ethnoarchaeological study of Aboriginal stone technology, I was thrilled to see several clear examples of notches being used. The inside edges of the notches were always employed for sharpening spear tips or shaving down small-diameter

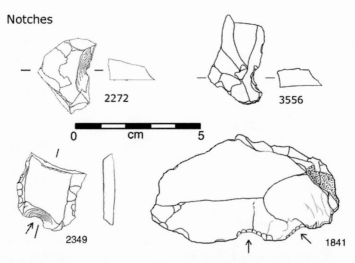

Figure 4.10. Notches and a denticulate from the Keatley Creek site. (From Hayden and Spafford 2000, p. 40, Figure 17; drawing by Suzanne Villeneuve)

Figure 4.11. An Aboriginal Australian at Papunya (Northern Territory) using a denticulate to shave down a spear shaft.

shafts of spears or other wooden objects (Figure 4.11; see also Figure 1.1). Notches are simple, very effective ways of rejuvenating a dull edge or creating a small but highly effective cutting edge for wood or bone working. To iterate, they are so simple that they often go unnoticed by analysts.

The French use the term *denticulé* to refer to a flake with more than one notch, no matter where it occurs on a flake. However, in North America the term carries the implication that there are a series of adjacent notches in a row—usually of small size—like a serrated edge. Thus I would prefer to use a separate term from denticulate for flakes with more than one large notch. "Multi-notch" is a term that would seem to avoid any implication of serrated series of small notches.

On the North American Northwest plateau, I have distinguished between the large type of notches defined by the French and smaller, intentionally made notches half a centimeter or less in size. The smaller sizes would be unsuitable for working wood shafts with diameters like spears, but could be effectively used on smaller shafts of wood or bone such as arrow shafts, basketry warps, or the tips of bone awls. Small, serrated series of notches are generally assumed to have been used as saws—perhaps on fish, meat, or wood (Figure 4.12).

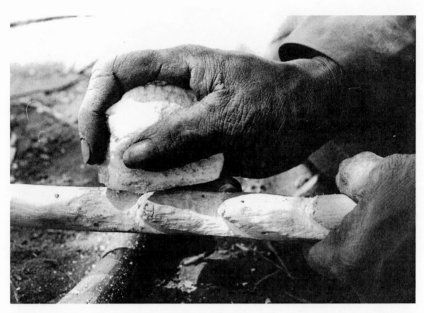

Figure 4.12. An Aboriginal Australian at Papunya (Northern Territory) using an unretouched flake to saw out the shape of the barbs on a spear. It is thought that finely denticulated flakes similar to this may have been used for comparable purposes.

Burinations

A good reason for examining flake edges by holding the edge pointed at your face is to detect possible burinations. Instead of removing flakes from one of the faces of a flake, burins remove long segments of an edge with a single blow to an end of the flake when it is held with the edge (rather than the face) pointed toward you. The removal of a long segment of the edge is called a burination, and the flake that comes off is called burin spall (Figure 4.13). Preparation of a striking platform at the end of a flake is often required—either by truncating the end, breaking the end, or removing a burin from the end to create a small narrow striking platform for a second burin removal. Resharpening can be accomplished by successive removal of burin spalls from the same striking platform at the end of the flake.

Dihedral burins are burinations from opposite side edges of a flake so that the burin scars come to a point at the flake's distal end and are thought to have been used to deeply score bone. However, on the basis of the edge morphology of the sides of burinations, which are close to 90-degree angles and are slightly concave, there is a strong possibility that it was the sides of most burins that were the main working edges.

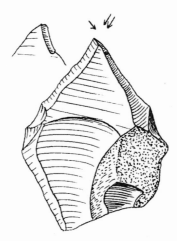

Figure 4.13. A burin from the Middle Paleolithic in France. The arrows indicate the direction of the burin blows that removed the edges lengthwise. The removed edges are known as burin spalls. (From Bordes 1961, Plate 34:11)

This is a use proposed by François Bordes many years ago, but burin-like edges are something that I also observed being used by Australian Aborigines. Burins tend to be popular in specific regions and periods in the world and are much less common or absent in many other traditions. They are especially common in the European Upper Paleolithic and the North American Paleoindian periods.

Battering

Battering may not technically be an intentional modification of flakes. It is more a byproduct of use, but not exactly use-wear either, so I am including it here. Battering seems to occur in two use contexts that I am familiar with. The first is the use of stone flakes that were employed as wedges to split wood, bone, or antler. The second is the use of more or less pointed stones against other stones—for instance, in making or rejuvenating grinding stone surfaces.

The use of flakes as wedges results in one or both edges being crushed (the edge placed in the material to be split, and the opposite edge receiving the impact blows), often with step fractures extending along both faces of a main edge and frequently with similar crushing and removals from the opposite edge. Flakes chosen for wedges often have two relatively straight edges along the lateral sides of the flake (Figure 4.14). These are referred to as battered or splintered pieces, or *pièces esquillées* in France.

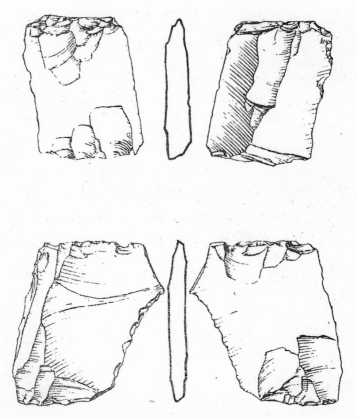

Figure 4.14. Two examples of battered pieces (or *pièces esquillées*) illustrating the battering on top and bottom edges, the original thin flake morphology, and the minimal removal of flakes from the battering. These characteristics indicate the use of these items as wedges that were struck with soft or hard hammers. Original figures courtesy of François Bordes.

Pieces of stone used to create grinding surfaces or other ground stone usually have crushing on points or edges. Pieces of quartzite with a few simple flakes removed to make a pointed edge, or even old ground stone adzes, could be used to repeck grinding surfaces. Chopper-like tools used to shape ground stone objects like metates also display crushing on their working edges (see Figure 1.2).

Bifacial Rotary Retouch

Some flakes exhibit flaking patterns that only make sense if the tools were meant to be used for piercing materials in a rotary fashion (Figure 4.15). Such tools usually are shaped by hard hammer retouch on both faces that progressively narrows and elongates two sides of a flake to a

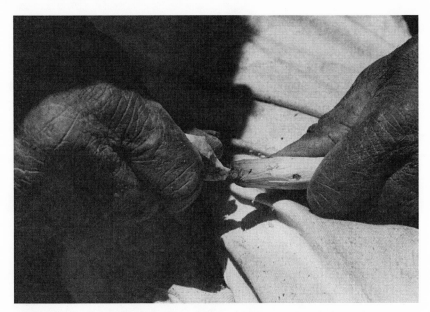

Figure 4.15. An Aboriginal Australian indenting a spear butt with an unretouched pointed flake at Papunya (Northern Territory). The butts of spears were indented in order to firmly seat the butt on the hook of spearthrowers. This is one possible use for retouched tools with the same general morphology such as borers and perforators.

point. These include heavy-duty "borers" and lighter "perforators," or drills, the latter of which is usually pressure flaked (Figure 4.16). Very fine, almost needle-sharp pointed flakes for piercing skin or hides can be made by minimal pressure flaking of naturally pointed flakes.

Figure 4.16. A Mousterian example of a piercer that could have been used in a manner similar to that shown in Figure 4.15. (From Bordes 1961, Plate 35:12)

Intentional Breaks

Intentional breaks are another rarely recognized type of modified flake tool. I have seen many examples of flakes or broken tools (even bifaces!) that were intentionally broken. They displayed points of impact on the break faces as well as use-wear along the break edges. The resulting edges are similar to the edges on the sides of burins and they are just as effective for planing wood. Intentional breaks may be considered as alternate strategies for creating burin-like edges close to 90 degrees. In addition, I recorded these kinds of edges being very effectively used by Australian aboriginals for scraping wood shafts of spears or other shaft objects (Figure 4.17). They would be equally effective in shaving down pieces of bone or antler. As mentioned previously, it is also possible that they could have been used to remove the epidermis and/or membrane in wet scraping hides since contemporary hideworkers prefer right-angled metal edges for these tasks. In these cases the use-wear should be distinctive.

Figure 4.17. An Aboriginal Australian at Papunya (Northern Territory) using the broken edge of a flake to effectively shave down the shaft of a spear. Flakes could be purposely broken in order to use such edges. Burinated edges exhibit similar highly effective edges for shaving round wood, bone, or antler.

Utilized Flakes versus Trampled Flakes

In design analysis, as in more traditional lithic analyses, it is critical to determine which modifications to tools were intentional and which modifications were not. Aside from the battered pieces discussed above, unintentionally modified flakes generally take the form of utilized and trampled flakes. Besides knowing that a flake was used because it was intentionally modified for use, primary flakes sometimes exhibit visible wear traces—indicating they were used as tools. Unfortunately, trampled pieces of debitage can sometimes look very similar to utilized flakes and may be difficult to distinguish from them.

If you have a source of lithic material (or thick glass like champagne bottles), the best way to understand the range of variation of both utlized flakes and trampled flakes is to use a number of flakes to shave down wood and bone until some small flake damage occurs. Make notes and drawings of what this looks like and the range of variation that exists. Then take a handful of debitage and toss it on the ground, spending some time to walk over it (or jump on it) until you've done enough damage. Then look at those flakes and record the damage characteristics.

Some useful guidelines are that small flakes removed from use rarely are more than one millimeter in length on cryptocrystalline materials; the use-generated flakes tend to be concentrated in one use zone of the edge; they tend to be oriented perpendicular to the edge; and they are more or less continuous. Trampling, on the other hand, is often— but not always—more irregularly spread along edges; involves a larger range of sizes of flakes (including some larger than one millimeter, especially if large animals have done the trampling); often have varying orientations; and often are characterized by small break morphologies. "Half-moon" breaks are especially characteristic of thin edges. Note again that thin edges are highly susceptible to trampling damage. If an edge has only one or two diminutive flake scars, this is insufficient indication to call it "used."

Other Sources of Edge Modification

Other sources of flake modification include hafting, damage from archaeologists' trowels and plows, solifluction, and heat cracking.

Hafting

Hafting can be reflected in edge modifications such as the use of opposing notches for binding the notched piece to a haft (e.g., with arrowheads); the presence of tangs; the removal of bulbs of percussion; the abrupt changes in resharpening and edge profiles (e.g., with some bifaces resharpened down to nubs); in traces of resin or changes in surface coloration; in abrasion due to loose hafts; in standardized widths; and, as discussed above, in Quina type of retouch, steep retouch, or the use of backing. Size may also be used as a criterion, as with microblades.

It is important to carefully distinguish between semi-abrupt or abrupt retouch made on a flake for the use of that edge versus retouch made in order to fit a flake into a haft. A flake tool that has been modified for prehension—for example, with blunting to avoid cuts when holding a flake—also needs to be distinguished (where possible) from resharpening for use on materials being worked. Similarly, notches made for hafting should be carefully distinguished from notches made in order to employ their edges for cutting or shaving hard materials. Usually, notches for hafting have bifacial flake removals that facilitate their identification.

Hafting can have profound effects on tool morphologies, tool use-lives or replacement rates, and assemblage characteristics so that detecting hafting is important. For instance, hafting can:

- Explain why certain tool types have unusually standardized widths (to fit the hafts.
- Influence the morphology of tool types.
- Reduce the amount of raw material needed for tasks.
- Change the type of raw material suitable for tasks.
- Change the proportion of tools related to tasks in the overall assemblage due to long, active use-lives.
- Result in more intensive resharpening of tools.
- Change retouch characteristics of tool types.

Trowel and Plow Damage

Trowel damage can often be easily identified if there is any patina, staining, or dirt in the pores of flaked stones. In contrast to the discoloration from these sources, recent damage from troweling shows up as a fresh flake scar lacking staining, dirt, or patina. On the other hand, flakes removed from edges by plows usually stay in the ground for some time, and thus the flake scars often become discolored with dirt adhering to ancient as well as modern surfaces. This can create problems for archaeologists working in plowed sites since plows can remove good-sized pieces from flake edges, thus mimicking notches or scrapers. In these instances the key is to look for lines of iron oxide on the faces of flakes. They often lead right to the point of impact of the flakes removed from the edges. Sometimes any lines from the contact of the plow against the face of the flake are enough to warrant excluding those flakes from analysis, since their integrity may have been compromised.

Solifluction

Solifluction effects are usually much easier to recognize since the frost heaves and soil movements tend to abrade the edges of flakes, as well as remove flakes from the edges due to active contact with other stones in the soil.

Heat Cracking, Crazing, and Potlids

Although not technically modifications to edges, these features do occur on faces of flakes that are being analyzed. They are caused by exposing homogeneous cryptocrystalline and fine crystalline stones to high heat in fires. This is usually done inadvertently (e.g., by making a fire in a place where there is lithic debitage) or as a casual tossing of an exhausted tool or piece of debitage into a fire. Fine crack lines or crazing can form on the surface of these pieces, as well as—or instead of— potlids. Potlid fractures are small, circular, bowl-shaped fractures that pop off the surface of flakes exposed to heat. They don't have points of impact or other fracture features that characterize intentional reduction strategies.

In addition to these features, pieces that have been exposed to fire often exhibit color changes toward the reds and sometimes have blackened surfaces. Not much cultural meaning can usually be attributed to these features (except for controlled intentional heat treatment of some stones to make them better for flaking), but it is good to know what they are when undertaking analysis—even if just to eliminate them from subsequent studies for use-wear or residue analysis.

UNMODIFIED TOOLS

As I indicated, there are sometimes good reasons to think that unmodified flakes have been selected and used as tools. These include pointed flakes from cores that have been carefully set up to produce pointed flakes that could be fitted to the end of a spear without any further modification. Examples include Levallois points and the similar Australian leilira points (Figure 4.18 left). Levallois points are recognized by most Middle Paleolithic archaeologists as probable spear points since they are difficult to make and resemble Mousterian points, which have the same identical shape but a bit of retouch along the sides to make them more pointed (Figure 4.18 center). In some assemblages there are flakes with a long, sharp cutting edge along one lateral side and a more or less right-angled edge on the opposite lateral edge that is covered with cortex. These are referred to as naturally backed knives. They seem to have been carefully selected by Neandertals since they occur far more frequently in Mousterian assemblages than would be expected by chance production (Figure 4.18 right).

Although not chipped stone, hammerstones, tent weights, anvils, fossils, and specially colored or shaped stones might be identified as objects that were used but lacked any modification (except for context) for the tasks they were used for.

SUMMARY

We have covered the basics of how to identify culturally modified stones from naturally occurring ones, how to separate tools from debitage, and how to identify different types of flake modifications or resharpenings. These artifacts and debitage comprise probably 95–99 percent of most lithic assemblages that you will ever deal with. I have tried to emphasize some of the types of edge modification that are frequently overlooked or misinterpreted by prehistorians: the notches, expedient knives, battered pieces, and intentional breaks. Recognition of what was done to a piece of stone is the basis for most stone tool typologies, but

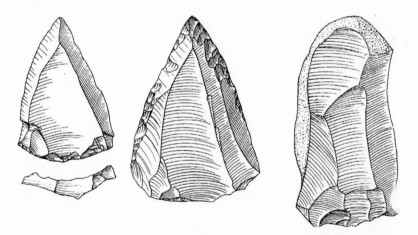

Figure 4.18. *Left.* Example of an unretouched tool type, a Levallois point (from Bordes 1961, Plate 9:3). *Center.* A Mousterian point type, essentially a Levallois point retouched to make a finer point (from Bordes 1961, Plate 9:8). *Right.* Another example of an unretouched tool type, a Mousterian naturally backed knife. The stippling on the left edge indicates cortex. These types of flakes occur with unusual frequencies in Mousterian assemblages, which is why they have been recognized as intentionally selected types of flakes for tool use similar to the unretouched flake used in Figure 4.12 (from Bordes 1961, Plate 37:15).

the creation of typologies varies enormously and will be addressed in Chapter 6.

We have not yet discussed the infrequent, specially shaped types of stone tools such as drills, projectile points, and bifaces. These are topics for the next chapter, together with a discussion of yet another fundamental aspect of lithic analysis: the underlying reduction strategies.

EXERCISE

If you can find a few thick champagne bottles or some old, thick ceramics, toilet bowls, or raw materials, or even quartzite or cryptocrystalline cobbles from a streambed, make some flakes. If you are using glass, be sure to wear leather gloves. Then try making scraper retouch, abrupt retouch, and a notch. Then try using an unretouched flake to shave a piece of hard wood and a piece of bone (uncooked is best) until you notice some use-wear developing.

Take some of the unused flakes outside and put them on the ground. Walk, jump, or dance on the flakes until you can notice some edge damage. Compare the trampled edge damage with the use-wear damage you produced previously. What systematic differences can you detect? Do you think you could accurately distinguish the two in an assemblage of archaeological materials? What percent of the time?

ADDITIONAL READINGS

Bordes, François. 1965. Utilisation possible des côtés des burins. *Funderichte aus Schwaben* 17:3–4. While most prehistorians assumed that the working part of Upper Paleolithic burins was the "bit" at the proximal end of the burin blow (as the name "burin" implies), Bordes argues that the side edges of burins were actually the active part of the tool in many cases.

Dibble, Harold L. 1995. Middle Paleolithic Scraper Reduction: Background, Clarification, and Review of the Evidence to Date. *Journal of Archaeological Method and Theory* 2:299–368. French prehistorians classified scrapers of the Middle Paleolithic into many types based on the shape of the retouched edge and the location of the retouched edge on the flake. In this classic analysis, Dibble shows that almost all of these separate "types" were actually different stages of resharpening of a single basic scraper type.

Hayden, Brian, and Margaret Nelson. 1981. The Use of Chipped Lithic Material in the Contemporary Maya Highlands. *American Antiquity* 46:885–898. This article summarizes some of the most important results about the use of chipped stone in contemporary Maya communities, notably in regard to the use of chopper-like tools to work vesicular basalt in the making of metates.

Tindale, Norman. 1965. Stone Implement Making Among the Nakako, Ngadadjara, and Pitjandjara of the Great Western Desert. *Records of the South Australian Museum* 15:131–164. This is a classic article describing stone tool making and use in Australia, specifically focusing on the hafted chipped stone flake adze. Tindale was able to document the progressive changes in tool morphology as the hafted flakes were repeatedly resharpened (Figure 4.5), a feature that Dibble argued also characterized Middle Paleolithic scrapers.

CHAPTER 5

TIER 2: BASIC REDUCTION STRATEGIES AND SPECIAL TYPES

As previously discussed, design theory is especially suited to understanding specialized tools in some detail, although these are often some of the least frequent tool types in assemblages. To consider each specialized tool type in detail would extend this book beyond its limits, but a few general points can be made (as was done with end scrapers). Arrowheads, too, merit some comments since they feature so prominently in many lithic analyses. However, the bulk of this chapter will be devoted to some of the less obvious features of stone tools—notably, reduction strategies. Reduction strategies are the ways in which raw lithic materials were knapped to obtain useful flakes, bifaces, or "core tools." They can provide some unique insights into design constraints.

SPECIALIZED TOOLS: PROJECTILE POINTS

Arrowheads, or projectile points, are probably the single most important artifact in generating interest in stone technology in North America. For many laypeople they are virtually synonymous with stone technology. Yet archaeologically they are not frequently encountered in the systematic excavation of prehistoric sites. It is undoubtedly the carefully shaped, symmetrical, easy-to-recognize features of most arrowheads—as well as their hunting and warfare implications—that appeal to people. Aside from the prestige "eccentric" forms produced by state-level lithic traditions like the Maya (Figure 5.1) or the elegant pressure-flaked knives, there are very few artifacts that were as carefully shaped as pro-

Figure 5.1. This Mayan eccentric from Tikal is a remarkable example of skilled flintknapping by a highly trained specialist producing an impressive prestige object.

jectile points. Late Neolithic Scandinavian flint daggers (Figure 5.2) and those from Çatal Höyük provide other classic examples of elaborately pressure-flaked prestige items. In addition to projectile points, bifaces and drills are perhaps the most widespread specialized tool types in many areas of the world, but they too generally constitute a very low percentage of tool assemblages.

Figure 5.2. Other examples of skilled flintknapping by specialists are the Late Neolithic Scandinavian daggers that imitate in stone the form of bronze daggers. This example is a reproduction made by Errett Callahan (length is 19.5 centimeters).

A word of caution is warranted in the use of the terms "spear point" or "projectile point," especially when referring to the larger varieties in North America. Large points may not have been projectile points at all. They could have been used on thrusting spears or they could even have been simply hafted onto short handles and used as bifacial knives (Figure 5.3). So beware of assuming that all points were projectiles. To make things even more complicated, Stanley Ahler has shown that some spearpoints were part of removable foreshafts of spears and were detached from the main spear shafts to be used as knives after kills.

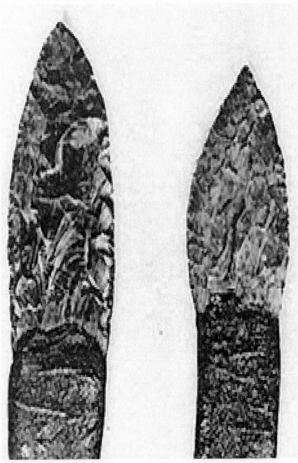

Figure 5.3. Hafted bifacial knives—like this ethnographic example of a Yurok fish knife—often resemble very large spear points. In this case the bifacial form indicates that these knives were probably used for butchering very large numbers of fish. (From Goddard 1903, Plate 3)

Since simple hammerstones are far too crude to shape flakes of stone into specific forms, special flakers that required special techniques and considerable practice were employed in the production of projectile points. Not everyone could make a good-looking projectile point. Making carefully shaped points (as well as drills and eccentrics) involved pressure flaking, whereas billet flaking (discussed below) was used for most bifaces or the initial stages of projectile point manufacture.

While most projectile points were carefully shaped using pressure flaking, it also needs to be recognized that some traditions used minimally retouched or unretouched pointed flakes (such as the Mousterian Levallois points or the Australian leilira points). Some projectile points were unretouched microblades along the projectile sides and tip; some used backed geometrical microlithis like trapezes or triangles; and some—like the chipped stones embedded in human bones at the Nilotic site of Sahaba—turned out to be the tips of drills or small scrapers or even unretouched debitage that had been expediently repurposed for use as projectile tips. In addition, some projectile tips were made of bone or antler, and probably the vast majority of projectile tips throughout the ethnographic world were simply made of hard woods. More grist for design theory enthusiasts.

Why was stone used for projectile points? No stone projectile points were used throughout New Guinea and in most of Australia, but this didn't prevent people from hunting or fighting. If stone-tipped projectiles were so effective, why didn't people use stone-tipped spears and arrows much earlier? And why didn't our ancestors use stone-tipped spears for the first two million years or so of hunting-gathering existence? The answer still remains to be determined. Experiments by Nicole Waguespack and her colleagues indicate that the penetration advantages of stone-tipped projectiles are not very significant. They conclude that social and symbolic factors may have led to the adoption of stone projectile points. By contrast, Christopher Ellis has found a very strong relationship between stone projectile points and the hunting of large mammals (over forty kilograms) and use in warfare, which he attributes to the greater internal damage done by stone projectiles—thus making them more lethal. This has since been verified and seems a more compelling explanation.

Spears or Arrows?

A surprising amount of work has been done by archaeologists to determine whether stone projectile points were used on spears or arrows. The costs and benefits of each system lend themselves very well to design theory analyses.

Many people may assume that the bow and arrow system was naturally superior to the atlatl (spearthrower) and spear (or long dart) system. However, given a little reflection, this is far from evident. In fact, the spearthrower and dart system remained in use in a number of areas of North America until Europeans arrived, even though people certainly knew of the bow and arrow. It had been adopted in the Arctic beginning around 3000 B.C.E. and somewhat later in other areas. In the Old World, the bow and arrow seem to be considerably older, at least as old as the Mesolithic rock art that depicted them. The Aztecs and Maya continued to use *atlatls* (an Aztec word) and darts, especially in war (as the Spaniards quickly discovered). Other groups used both the atlatl and bow together, and archaeologically—even where the bow and arrow eventually became the exclusive weapon—there was usually a transition period when atlatls and bows coexisted, often for a millennium or more. If the advantages of the bow and arrow were so great, then why did it take so long for groups to stop using atlatls and darts? And why did some groups never adopt them?

The bow and arrow seems to have the advantages of increased accuracy and increased range, in contrast to atlatls and darts. The bow and arrow is also easier to learn to use and easier to use in dense forests or under cramped conditions like ambush hunting. Hunters can also carry more arrows with them than spears, and arrows involve less material to make than spears. Making arrowheads is also easier than making spear points.

However, there are also some key disadvantages to the bow and arrow. Just making a bow with an adequate bowstring and fletched arrows involves more time and skill than the making of a simple spearthrower and long dart or spear. A spearthrower could be as simple as a stout branch with a side branch cut to form a hook. Spears also are much heavier than arrows and thus have a much deadlier impact on animals. Spears are therefore more effective in bringing down large animals if this is the goal. Of even greater importance is the fact that atlatls are much more reliable than bows and require little maintenance or care. Bowstrings, on the other hand, are susceptible to breaking—especially if misused. If they are made of tendons or hide strips, bowstrings can be unusable if they become wet from rain, snow, or traversing streams. Moreover, only one hand is required to fire an atlatl dart and atlatls can be especially effective when used on foot in the open with herds of large animals, or in conflicts with dense throngs of combatants. Thus, depending on the constraints in given situations, the atlatl might well complement the bow and arrow, or might even be the preferred weapon in hunting and warfare.

Consequences

The adoption of the bow and arrow had a number of effects on other aspects of culture. As several authors have suggested, enhanced accuracy and range may well have increased the ability to kill more animals and may well have provided advantages in armed conflicts. These effects should be manifest in higher faunal frequencies after the adoption of the bow and arrow, and perhaps local extirpation of large game animals and greater emphasis on smaller mammals. Such changes in archaeological faunas could easily be misinterpreted as resulting from climate changes or other factors.

Moreover, like the adoption of the gun by indigenous groups in North America, the military advantages provided by the bow and arrow could have also resulted in major population expansions and movements (as with Numic groups in the Great Basin after the introduction of the bow and arrow). It has even been suggested that the change from highly patterned technologies that emphasized formal types to more expedient technologies may have been due to the adoption of the bow and arrow, rather than a reduction in mobility. Thus the consequences of adopting the bow and arrow could have had far-reaching effects beyond a simple improvement in projectile technology.

REDUCTION STRATEGIES

In addition to specially designed tools, important insights into the design process can be inferred from the way blocks of stone were knapped or reduced. Once a person has decided on the design of a tool he or she wants to produce—whether simply to obtain a sharp cutting edge or to drill holes in shell beads—the next step is to determine how to transform raw stone into a usable shape for the tool. In contrast to pottery, which creates shapes by adding lumps of clay together, flint knapping is by its very nature a subtractive or reductive technique for shaping things. There are a number of basic ways that stone can be reduced to a desired shape using chipping techniques, and the reduction strategies chosen can indicate some important things about the design constraints for various solutions. For instance, reduction techniques can be influenced by the type of material that is available and suitable; mobility, transport, and time constraints; risks of failure; the need to conserve material; the quantity of materials needing to be processed; and probably other factors. Identifying reduction strategies therefore plays an important part in understanding lithic assemblages.

There are six basic types of reduction strategies encountered in most lithic assemblages, as well as a number of regional variations.

- Hard hammer block core reduction.
- Blade reduction.
- Bipolar reduction.
- Bifacial reduction.
- Levallois reduction.
- Pressure reduction.

On very rare occasions, thin pieces of stone may also be reduced by radial fracturing, such as occurs when you throw a rock at a piece of plate glass. Different fracture mechanics and different fracture features tend to characterize most of the above reduction strategies. These will be mentioned in our discussions, but if you want to know more about these strategies, a detailed understanding of fracture mechanics—a subfield of its own—should be acquired from other publications. It is also crucial to emphasize that reduction strategies do not usually characterize entire assemblages. They characterize tools used in specific tasks or groups of tasks.

Hard Hammer Block Core Reduction

Block core reduction (aka amorphous cores, expedient cores, multi-directional cores) is the most common form of reduction throughout the world in most time periods. Anyone can generally obtain flakes from a block core and make the sharp edges needed for basic survival skills. It consists simply of using a hard hammer—a hard, tough stone—to remove one or more initial cortex-bearing flake(s) in order to create a striking platform from which subsequent flakes are detached according to the type of flake one needs. The resulting flakes and cores have all the classic conchoidal ("cone" fracture) characteristics depicted for intentional flakes: pronounced bulbs of percussion, ripples, and fissures. The cone shape is produced by "blunt indenter" mechanics. Flakes can be removed from block cores in a relatively random fashion (using whatever striking platform seems most suitable for producing the desired size and shape of flakes), or the cores can be intentionally set up with a flaking strategy that produces a directional orientation of flakes from one (unidirectional) or two (bidirectional) ends of cores.

Block core reduction tends to characterize tasks in which the quantity being processed is very low or occasional, with few or no time constraints and no immediate dire consequences if the task is not completed. They are also used when flexibility of obtained flake types is important—that is, making whatever type of flake you need for a specific task rather than being stuck with a predetermined type of flake (like microblades) that may not be suited for your task at hand. Interestingly, randomly oriented block cores seem to dominate sedentary or semi-sedentary hunter-gatherer and horticultural settlements, such as those of most complex hunter-gatherers and most village agriculturalists. This probably reflects the stocking of core material at these sites and the occasional and varied nature of most tasks—resulting in the retrieval of a core and the removal of one or more expedient flakes for the immediate task at hand, rather than preparing specific blanks ahead of time for expected future needs far away from sources of tool raw material.

I also found it interesting in my analysis of stone tools derived from block core reduction at the Keatley Creek site that a high proportion of the tools were on small flakes, often only 2–3 centimeters in length. This, together with many recycled and multi-type tools and the uniformly small size of debitage, undoubtedly reflected shortages in the amount of stone material stockpiled at this semi-sedentary winter village.

Blade Reduction

Technically, simple blades (flakes that are more than twice as long as they are wide) can be removed from block cores if one is careful and sets up the core properly in a directional fashion. However, the results are variable and the edges not reliably straight. In order to consistently produce very straight and very long blades, special reduction techniques are required together with special skills and special equipment. In the Upper Paleolithic, blade cores were shaped a bit like a short boat with the striking platform corresponding to the prow of the boat deck. A "crested blade" was the first to be removed from a properly prepared core. The crested blade would correspond to the tip of the prow and the front keel of the boat. This blade was not usually used, but it set up long ridges at the sides of the blade scar that guided subsequent blade removals. An intermediate punch of bone or antler was used to make the fracture travel as far as possible.

Other blade core shapes were used in areas like Mesoamerica, where cores were more bullet or cone shaped and worked in a circular pattern. A similar technique was used in the production of microblades (less than 1.2 centimeters wide), although very small microblades (less than 0.5 centimeter) like those in the Far East, India, Northeast Asia, southern Africa, and the American Northwest could be produced with a long pressure flaker as well. Larger Mesoamerican obsidian blades could also be produced by long pressure flakers fitted to chests or foot levers.

Microblades

The production and use of microblades is a notable development in the lithic technology of almost every inhabited continent of the world. Explaining why it occurred is one of the more intriguing and daunting questions that still needs to be answered.

Microblades always seem to be used in composite hafted tools, whether spears, arrows, sickles, or knives. It has been suggested that microblades slotted into the sides of antler points would be even better than stone projectile points at penetrating deeply into animals and creating more hemorrhaging. The antler spearheads would also be much more resistant to shattering on impact, and even if the side bladelets broke or became dislodged, they could be easily replaced. These advantages might more than compensate for the extra time, effort, and skill needed to make projectile points of antler with microblades slotted in the sides. A number of these antler projectiles with their microblades still in place have been recovered from Mesolithic deposits in Scandinavia and Siberia, and ethnographic accounts document similar arrangements of bladelet-like flakes still in use historically in Australia (Figure 5.4).

Some microblades on the American Northwest Coast have been found end-hafted onto small pieces of wood about the size of popsicle

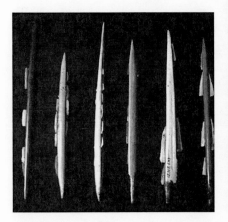
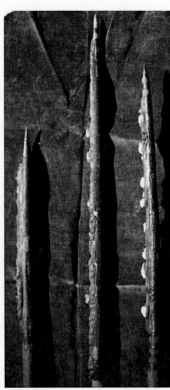

Figure 5.4. *Left.* Archaeological microliths found still hafted in their antler foreshafts from the Mesolithic of southern Sweden (displayed in the Lund Museum). *Right.* Ethnographic examples of "death spears" showing the use of microflakes on spear foreshafts. Courtesy of the South Australian Museum.

sticks. These were apparently very effective for cutting through salmon skins in butchering, like little disposable razors. Just as intriguing as understanding the origin and spread of microlithic technology is the challenge of understanding why it disappeared in many places—such as Australia and the American Northwest—where it was replaced by pressure-flaked projectile points and other kinds of cutting tools.

Oversized Blades

At the other end of the size spectrum, in the French and Iberian Neolithic and the Bulgarian Chalcolithic, some exceptionally large and long flint blades (up to forty centimeters long) were produced that appear to have been status items (Figure 5.5). Their exhausted cores almost resembled

Figure 5.5. A late Neolithic blade core from Le Grand Pressigny in western central France (length is 25 centimeters). The very long blades from these cores were highly valued and traded hundreds of kilometers to the Netherlands, the Pyrenees, and the Alps. Such large blades appear to have been prestige items.

handaxes or Levallois-like blade cores with only a few large blades that could be removed from a single core. The exceptional size, fragility, lack of use, required skill, and funerary contexts of these blades argue in favor of seeing them as prestige items with strong symbolic connotations—one of the few lithic instances where this can be established with some certainty.

It should be iterated here that the term "blades" is used in some areas of North America to refer to bifaces; however, as will become evident below, bifaces are technologically very different creatures from the blades we are discussing here. In order to avoid confusion, I would strongly urge that use of the term "blade" be restricted to the definition employed here, which is the most common usage in the English-speaking world.

Costs and Benefits of Blades

As discussed in Chapter 3, the development of macroblades—and the not inconsiderable skills required to produce them—makes a good deal of sense in terms of the need for filleting a high volume of meat in a short period of time, as well as the high number of resharpenings needed for scraping large quantities of ungulate hides. Others have suggested that high-mobility conditions and limited transport capabilities may also have been factors favoring the production and use of blades, due to tool designs that favored multiple resharpenings and the production of basic flake types for a range of different tasks (such as butchering, skin scraping, woodworking, and bone working). In effect, blades can be used for all these purposes and lend themselves especially well to resharpening using scraper retouch (including end scrapers), invasive retouch, abrupt retouch (truncations, backed pieces), burinations, and special shaping (e.g., for projectile points). In addition, according to some authors, removing a series of blades from cores produces more cutting edge per weight of raw material than any other major reduction technique. This, however, depends entirely on the width of the blades versus the size of the flakes produced by the two techniques.

Nevertheless, the use of blade reduction comes at the cost of procuring high-grade cryptocrystalline raw material and the development of the skills and tools required to successfully use this technique. The remaining blade core is also relatively large and useless. Hence blade production can indicate a significant cost, including obtaining suitable raw material for tools. It is also clear that not everyone—or not every adult—had the skills to use blade reduction techniques to produce good blades. Thus using this reduction technique also requires groups with enough people for someone to be able to learn the necessary skills to make blades.

In sum, there appear to be a number of different design constraints that can lead to lithic traditions involving blade reduction. High mobility and the need to conserve raw material may be two of those constraints, but they do not account for the production of blades in the largely sedentary communities of the Mesoamerican Classic and Post-Classic, the French and Iberian Neolithic, or the Bulgarian Chalcolithic. The tanning of a large number of ungulate hides and the filleting of a large amount of meat for drying and storage provide other constraints that can be expected to make blade production a key part of attractive tool solutions. Specialized and standardized hafting requirements can also make blade production an attractive solution, as with the production of gunflints for flintlocks.

Bipolar Reduction

In contrast to the special skill required for making blades, almost anyone can use bipolar reduction techniques effectively and there are few other real constraints to obtaining flakes by bipolar reduction. Bipolar reduction is one of the earliest reduction strategies in the archaeological record, and perhaps the *first* reduction strategy developed even before the Oldowan. It is extremely simple to use, as simple as cracking nuts with a stone (which even chimpanzees do). Yet products of bipolar reduction are very frequently overlooked and even unrecognized by many lithic analysts, who frequently classify bipolar flakes and cores among simple debitage. Thus it is worth your while to become much more familiar with this type of reduction by doing a fair amount of it yourself (see the exercise).

Bipolar Mechanics and Identification

What is bipolar reduction? Bipolar reduction simply involves placing a piece of raw material (the target) on an anvil stone and using a hammerstone to split the target stone. The technique can be used on any shape of stone—even broken tools—but it is especially suitable for flaking small round pebbles that are too small to easily flake with direct, handheld, hard hammer percussion. The fracture mechanics involved are different from conchoidal fractures in that the fractures tend to be flat rather than undulating and there is no pronounced "bulb" of percussion (often none at all); there is only a point of impact. These major fractures are typical of "sharp indenter" mechanics.

In addition, repeated hammering is usually required to split pebbles and remove series of flakes. This usually results in considerable crushing and multiple step fracturing at the points of percussion, as well as along adjacent edges (although these may be absent due to successive flake removals). As bipolar cores get more reduced, flakes can come off either side of the core, often resulting in bifacial flake scars. Flakes sometimes also come off the end resting on the anvil, thus creating a "bipolar" aspect of the cores—that is, flakes removed from opposite ends.

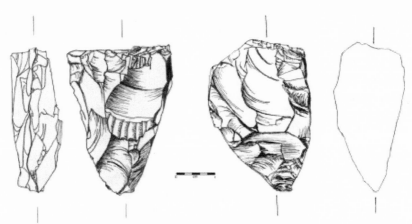

Figure 5.6. Two bipolar cores from Keatley Creek. (From Hayden and Spafford 2000, p. 47, Figure 24; drawing by Suzanne Villeneuve)

In highly reduced bipolar cores, there is no striking platform left, only an impact ridge or crest. The remaining cores do not always display all the characteristics I have described and identifying bipolar cores can take some practice. You should be able to identify many of these characteristics and some of the variability from the bipolar cores that you make in the exercise.

The flakes derived from bipolar cores tend to be relatively thin with low, sharp edge angles suitable for cutting skin, but these flakes are rarely retouched or modified. Because they lack bulbs of percussion, they are usually classified with shattered debitage. In addition, it can often be difficult to distinguish bipolar cores from battered pieces (*pièces esquillées*) since they can share many of the same characteristics. Basically, battered pieces are usually made of relatively thin flakes from which no one would expect to be able to obtain a usable flake (see Figure 4.12).

By contrast, bipolar cores usually are more chunky, clearly have had sizable flakes removed from `them, and have no indications of ever having been a thin flake to start with (Figure 5.6). All in all, since bipolar flakes can be difficult to recognize, bipolar cores are the best indicators of bipolar reduction in assemblages, and with good awareness and a bit of practice they can be easily identified. A word of warning is in order: midsections of bifaces (discussed next) can sometimes look like bipolar cores since thin flakes are removed bifacially from opposite ends, and edges for the removal of flakes sometimes exhibit step fracturing if the flint knapper did not properly prepare a striking platform or spoiled its execution—a common occurrence. Be alert for such situations. Careful inspection can usually resolve the issue.

Why Use Bipolar Reduction?

Bipolar reduction can be used as the major reduction strategy for working stone (see Peter White for New Guinea), but most often it is one of the main strategies for making expedient tools when good sources of large raw material are unavailable (see H. R. MacCalman and B. J. Grobbelaar for the Bushmen of Namibia). Quartz and quartzite are particularly resistant to being ground down by rivers during fluvial transport, so they tend to travel longer distances in streambeds or riverbeds and occur ubiquitously in many environments as pebbles that can be used by hunters or anyone else as expedient solutions for cutting needs. In settlements, when no suitable cores are available, large old or broken tools are often recycled and reduced by bipolar flaking to remove whatever small flakes can be gleaned from them. Thus bipolar reduction of pebbles or broken tools can indicate that better materials were not available or were reserved for more demanding tasks. On the other hand, bipolar reduction can also be used for exceptional materials like obsidian or crystal quartz, which may only be available in small sizes and limited amounts. Bipolar reduction, for example, was used in Kenya for the production of sharp flakes from quartz crystal in the ritual scarification of youths.

Because of the simplicity of bipolar reduction and the ubiquity of suitable materials, even children could conceivably produce sharp flakes this way and bipolar reduction was perhaps the first kind of flint knapping children were allowed to employ. By contrast, it seems doubtful that children in sedentary or semi-sedentary villages would have been allowed to smash up any of the valued lithic raw materials, since raw materials had to be brought in from many kilometers away and carefully used in order to last an entire season or two.

A special case of bipolar reduction is provided by the manufacture of spall tools that were widely used in northern North America for stretching and abrading hides. In these cases coarse-grained rounded cobbles, commonly of quartzite, were split using the bipolar technique in order to obtain a large oval cortex-bearing flake with a rounded working edge. The bipolar technique was chosen to produce these tools because it is uniquely suited to the splitting of round cobbles, yielding the desired shape of the tool with a relatively flat ventral face suitable for hafting (see Chapter 3).

Bifacial Reduction

Billet flaking employed in the making of bifaces constitutes a major type of reduction strategy. Bifacial reduction is primarily used for the production of bifaces. Before proceeding, however, a word needs to be said about the use of the term "biface." In France and elsewhere, biface refers to core-sized tools such as handaxes and thinner foliate pieces like the Solutrean flint laurel leaves. In North America there is an unfortunate tendency by some analysts to lump everything with bifacial retouch under the term "biface" including projectile points, bifacial knives (the equivalents of laurel leaves), bifacial scrapers, drills, and virtually any-thing that has some retouch on both faces. This results in a completely meaningless group of tools that mixes together different reduction strategies, different tasks, and different tool designs—a hodge-podge classification of artifacts from which nothing useful or intelligible can be extracted in any kind of analysis.

I therefore use the term "biface" in the European sense as pertain-ing to core-sized tools that have normally been produced by bifacial bil-let reduction. The one exception that I can think of would be very early Acheulian handaxes that were produced with hard hammers. As noted above in discussing blade reduction, the term "blade" should not be used to refer to bifaces.

The Mechanics of Bifaces

Bifacial reduction is characterized by the use of soft hammers or bil-lets—whether made of antler, hard wood, or in special cases soft stones. Soft hammers spread the impact of percussors over a wider area of the striking platform than hard hammer (stone) percussors. This results in a quite distinctive modified type of conchoidal fracture that lacks typi-cal focused and prominent bulbs of percussion, and sometimes other conchoidal features such as fissures. Instead there is a smooth fracture front that often extends across much of the length of the striking plat-form remnant.

When the core or biface surfaces lack much relief and are somewhat domed, the resulting fracture mechanics travel closer to the core/biface surface and farther across the piece, with a tendency to fan out into a teardrop shape (Figure 5.7 top). When the billet strikes close to the edge of the striking platform, the amount of striking platform removed with the flakes can be miniscule, much smaller than is generally possible with a hard hammer—although if the billet strikes far away from the core/bi-face edge, large sections of the striking platform will of course be re-moved, resulting in a very different, shorter, and distinctive flake type that looks in section like the Arabic letter "r" (which is why I refer to them as "r-billet" flakes; Figure 5.7 bottom). These are flaking mistakes that frequently ruin bifaces.

In general, debitage from biface manufacture and resharpening is highly distinctive and can usually be easily recognized on larger flakes. The upshot of successfully using bifacial reduction in the above fashion is that low edge angles can be maintained along the edges of bifaces over many resharpenings and minimal material is lost as platform rem-

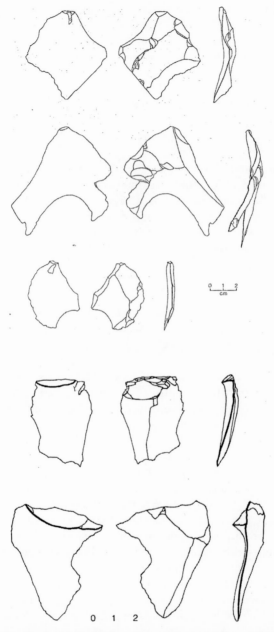

Figure 5.7. *Top.* Typical billet flakes from thinning bifaces illustrating characteristic small platforms, expanding sides, flake curvature, and thin cross-sections (from Hayden and Hutchings 1989, p. 246, Figure 6). *Bottom.* Examples of "r-billet" flakes with very large striking platforms, thick cross-sections, and short lengths. These were blunders in making bifaces, and in most cases probably ruined the biface (from Hayden and Hutchings 1989, p. 251, Figure 11).

nants. By contrast, hard hammer percussion requires large platforms for successful flake detachments and these rapidly increase the edge angles of striking platforms so that low edge angles cannot be maintained. Hard hammer percussion also creates thicker flakes that rapidly exhaust cores (Figure 5.8).

Costs and Benefits of Bifaces

Substantial costs are involved in effectively using bifacial reduction. First, material for suitable billets must be obtained and properly fashioned into a billet. Second, billets need to be carried around constantly for the resharpening of bifaces or for whatever tasks require obtaining thin flakes. Third, special skill and extended training are required to properly use bifacial reduction. Not every adult has the skill to make

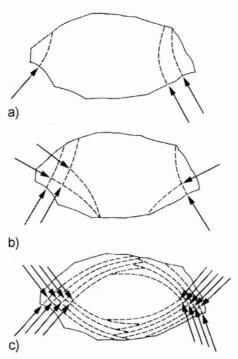

Figure 5.8. A schematic illustration showing how hard hammer reduction increases edge angles with successive flake removals and limits the number of flake removals per block of raw material. By contrast, billet flaking maintains or can reduce edge angles and makes possible many more flake removals from the same size material. (From Hayden and Hutchings 1989, p. 38, Figures 3–4)

acceptable bifaces. Fourth, high-quality raw material works best with bifacial reduction and needs to be procured. And fifth, billet flakes are relatively fragile and often break up on detachment. Thin bifaces, too, are prone to breakage.

Given these substantial costs, why is bifacial reduction adopted? The answer, again, can plausibly be related to the design constraint of the volume of material being processed. If you are an Australopithecine carrying around a core and you only manage to bring down an antelope once a month, then a few flakes knocked off the core with a hammerstone are probably enough to replace one or two spears, keep your spears sharp, and butcher your animal until you can get to a stone source to replenish the flakes that you used up.

But imagine (on the other hand) that you are a successful hunter killing an antelope about once or twice a week, and that for the last three years you have repeatedly run out of cryptocrystalline cores and flakes needed to sharpen or replace your spears and cut open your kills for butchering. You can only carry one small bag of flakes and a fist-sized block core on your forays without hindering your hunting pursuits, and the only good source of stone for your tools is two days walk away. You have had to resort to using grainy pebbles from local creeks for sharpening your spears and cutting through the hides in order to butcher the animals and save the skin. But these flakes don't sharpen your spears to fine penetrating points and they require a lot of effort to cut through the deerskins. You get so frustrated having to use these inferior materials that you try to figure out how you can avoid doing so. You could make more frequent trips to the quarries with high-quality raw material, but this would mean going far out of the way and getting fewer animals. You could go hunting less often, but you like eating meat too much and giving meat to others increases your status and attractiveness to the opposite sex. You could try to develop multiple uses of your tools so that you don't need to carry so much, but resharpening stone tools only goes so far and you need really sharp edges to cut through hides. Or you could try to find a way to extend the use-life of the material and tools that you carry.

How could you do this? Bifacial reduction is one of the most common answers, although blade and microblade reduction—sometimes used together with bifacial reduction—are other solutions. One other somewhat later solution was to create stone spear points that could be detached from the shaft and then be used as skinning knives.

Thus one of the big advantages of bifacial reduction is that many more resharpenings and usable flakes can be obtained with billet flaking from a bifacial core than with hard hammer percussion from a block core (Figure 5.8). As Robert Kelly has argued, under the constraints of limited access to raw materials due to high mobility and limited transport capacity, there is considerable pressure to maximize the usefulness of the stone material one has to carry. According to Kelly, bifacial reduction maximizes the amount of stone cutting edge while minimizing the amount of material needed to be carried. However, this interpretation is being disputed and Christopher Ellis has provided a nice overview of the costs and benefits of bifacial reduction in a Clovis context. I hasten to point out that high frequencies of use or processing volumes can also play an important role in adopting bifacial reduction, as with the bifacial fish knives used during major fish runs documented by James Hester in California.

Form Follows Function for Bifaces

In order to realize the advantage of using bifacial reduction, the cores must have special shapes. Not only would striking a flake from any shaped core with an antler billet be difficult, but it would not result in the desired economy of raw material or the desired features of flakes. Achieving the goal of repeatedly removing thin, invasive flakes requires three things: (a) low edge angles on the striking platforms; (b) properly shaped or prepared striking platforms strong enough to withstand the billet blow and transmit its force into the body of the core/biface; and (c) lenticular sections of the cores (see Figure 5.8). Because the edge angles are so low, they are relatively fragile and the point of impact frequently needs to be strengthened by small, semi-abrupt flake removals along the edge (and/or abrasion) in order to support the billet impact.

The result of these requirements is a finely crafted symmetrical biface like a handaxe or bifacial knife that can serve as both a tool and a continuing source of thin flakes particularly suited to cutting through hides. Such core-tools make a great deal of sense in terms of situations where there is a relatively frequent need for butchering and resharpening spears, arrows, or other equipment while engaged in hunting forays—and this is undoubtedly why bifaces occur in so many hunter-gatherer assemblages throughout the world. In addition to being very versatile and functionally enhanced by their pointed ends (bifacial knives are like Swiss Army knives of the Paleolithic), bifaces can be resharpened many times and when reduced in size could even be transformed into projectile points like Clovis spear points. The flakes removed from bifaces usually have razor sharp, low-angled edges around the entire perimeter of the flake (typically not the case with flakes from block cores). Being able to produce a number of these flakes when needed would be extremely useful for cutting through hides of medium and large game animals, due to the rapid dulling that often results from cutting through thick hair containing substantial dirt or the tough skins of salmon.

Thus, despite the costs, from a design perspective bifaces provide a very attractive solution to numerous constraints depending on the number of animals killed and the other factors discussed. Perhaps because of its long curated use-life and its principal use on hunting forays, bifaces or the pieces from them are generally not very numerous at residential habitation sites or base camps.

Bifaces as Prestige Items

Prehistorians without training in lithics have written a lot of nonsense about why symmetrical bifaces were made. Modern cognitive capacities, binary thought patterns, and cosmological concepts have all been invoked to explain the symmetry, form, and craftsmanship of Paleolithic bifaces. It even been suggested that handaxes were manufactured to show off skill in order to attract potential mating partners. From the preceding discussion, it should be apparent that these are highly dubious speculations and that far simpler explanations based on lithic fracture mechanics and design constraints are the more likely reasons for the form of bifaces. Form follows function. The lenticular sections and bilateral symmetries are simply the only way to get the maximum number of sharp flakes out of a piece of raw material using billet flaking.

Nevertheless, this does not mean that some bifaces could not have been used to advance social agendas or help solve sociopolitical problems as prestige objects. Bifaces just did not develop solely for those reasons. While the vast majority of bifaces were undoubtedly simple work tool solutions responding to practical problems, the fact that considerable skill and high-grade materials were necessary to make the best bifaces meant that some of them were suitable for use as prestige objects and objects of admiration. The most obvious examples are the oversized and over-thinned Solutrean laurel leaf bifaces (Figure 5.9), but other examples include the hafted bifacial knives found at Çatal Hoyuk and those used by the Maya and Aztecs for their human sacrifices. Ethnographically, oversized obsidian bifaces were used in competitive ritual feasting bouts in California as displays of wealth (Figures 5.10 and 5.11). On occasion complete bifaces of outstanding quality are sometimes found in burials or in pits as offerings, or possibly cached away and forgotten about, or hidden by someone who died or left the area before retrieving a prized item.

Exceptional bifaces are some of the few lithic artifacts to which we can attribute a sociopolitical role. Ground stone adzes are another type that lends itself to playing prestige roles, and (as previously noted) exceptionally long blades also seem to have been used as prestige items in some Upper Paleolithic and Neolithic cultures.

Sources of Confusion

A few words of caution need to be offered about identifying broken bifaces. First, in my analysis of bifaces from the Keatley Creek site, I have

Figure 5.9. One of the pinnacles of Upper Paleolithic flintworking in France was this large Solutrean laurel leaf. The photograph is of a cast of the largest laurel leaf biface known. It is 33 centimeters long and remarkably thin. It was far too delicate to be a functional tool and is one of the clearest examples of a lithic prestige item in the Upper Paleolithic.

Figure 5.10. Similar oversized bifaces were used as items of wealth ethnographically in California among the Yurok. Here two high-ranking members with headdresses of sea lion tusks are carrying their prized obsidian bifaces in ritual competitions. (From Goddard 1903, Plate 30)

found that pieces of bifaces—which had accidentally broken or reached the end of their use-lives—were often recycled, either by using an accidental break for shaving wood or by intentionally breaking off parts of the biface for the same purpose. The goal was to use the resulting break edges. Use of the broken pieces was evident from clear hard hammer impacts that had broken the biface, as well as from wear traces on the break edges.

As mentioned in the discussion of bipolar reduction, a word of caution is also warranted when bifaces have been broken into medial segments. These segments usually exhibit many of the same characteristics as bipolar cores so that it can sometimes be difficult to distinguish between them. Determining the direction of impact on the broken edges (breaks versus columnar fractures) helps distinguish bipolar cores from biface fragments.

Figure 5.11. Detailed views of the oversized obsidian bifaces ethnographically used as wealth items in California. The length of the largest is 33 centimeters. (From Kroeber 1925, Plate 2)

Levallois Reduction

The Levallois technique of producing flakes is a specialized technique that is related to—and in fact may have been derived from—bifacial reduction. Levallois reduction was common in many Acheulian and Middle Paleolithic assemblages in Europe and Africa and it appears sporadically elsewhere in the world, but is uncommon in the western hemisphere. The constraints that made Levallois reduction a popular solution in the Lower and Middle Paleolithic of the Old World seem to have changed by the later Paleolithic, with the development of new solutions like blade technology and the emergence of different constraints.

Basically, the Levallois technique for producing flakes consists of creating a domed upper surface on a core (sometimes called a turtle-back core) and then removing a large flake from the center of the dome. Hard hammer percussion is normally used to shape the core and remove the central flake. All fractures have a strong tendency to follow ridges, crests, or high points on cores like the top of a domed surface or the initial "keel" of a blade core. After removal of the large central flake, other flakes can then be removed from around the perimeter to refashion the domed surface and another large flake can be removed (Figure 5.12). Some people have suggested that the purpose for structuring the reduction in this fashion was to obtain the smaller peripheral flakes rather than a larger central flake from the central dome. However, it seems unlikely that the purpose of removing a large central flake was to continue removing smaller flakes from the periphery, since useful flakes could be easily removed from the periphery by rotating the core (as demonstrated by Mousterian disk cores).

The main advantage of Levallois reduction is that it provides a flake with a good cutting edge around the entire perimeter of the flake, yielding a maximum amount of cutting edge per flake—a flake that is also characterized by a fairly low, sharp edge angle. Like billet flakes from bifacial reduction, these central Levallois flakes make a good deal of sense in terms of transported tools that maximize the utility and effectiveness of the stone, which has to be carried under mobile conditions like hunting forays. However, the Levallois technique is very wasteful of material due to the many flakes of debitage produced by the shaping of the core just to remove a single useful flake or two. While some of the peripheral preparation flakes may have have been used as tools, their frequent small size makes it more likely that the main objective was to produce a large central flake (Figure 5.12). Since the technique wastes a lot of stone material to produce a few optimally useful flakes, it may have only been used at locations where there was an abundance of raw material.

The technique requires fairly sophisticated planning in the preparation of the cores and considerable skill for the detachment of the central flake, as you will find out if you ever try to produce a Levallois flake. This consideration alone should raise your level of respect for the hominins who made these tools, as well as the bifaces with which they were sometimes associated (e.g., the Mousterian of the Acheulian tradition). In fact, Levallois cores are very similar to key aspects of the Acheulian bifaces. If you imagine holding a handaxe up to eye level and looking down its length from the butt end so that you see its lenticular shape, this is exactly what a Levallois core would ideally look like. If

Figure 5.12. A typical Levallois core from the French Middle Paleolithic showing the peripheral preparatory flake removals and the large central flake removal (length is eight centimeters). A Levallois flake approximating the size of the flake from the core is at right.

you remove a large flake from the butt of the biface (taking off the central, domed—lenticular—top part from one face), you would have a Levallois flake. It is probably no coincidence, then, that Levallois reduction is so frequently associated with Acheulian bifaces at the outset.

Pressure Reduction

The use of pressure flaking to remove flakes and shape tools like projectile points, eccentrics, drills, and prestige knives is a relatively late development that first appeared in the Upper Paleolithic of Europe about twenty thousand years ago but quickly spread throughout the inhabited world. It consists of using a soft indenter—usually a pointed piece of antler, bone, hard wood, or copper—to remove pressure flakes from blades, block core flakes, or thinned bifaces. Pressure flakes are like miniature biface reduction flakes, but usually not much more than a centimeter in length (at most) with the same characteristics in the impact area as billet flakes, only smaller. Like billet flakes, they require special platform preparation and are thin and can travel across the entire width of pieces being worked, but usually break up after a short distance due to their thinness. Pressure reduction debitage is therefore fairly distinctive and relatively easy to recognize, while the tools made by this reduction strategy tend to be infrequent or rare—except for microblades produced from microblade cores by pressure flaking.

Advantages and Disadvantages of Pressure Flaking

The major advantages of using pressure flaking are that consistently low edge angles can be created and maintained for cutting or piercing tools, and that pressure flakes remove little amounts of material in each resharpening—with many resharpenings being possible. The serrated edges that naturally result from a series of pressure flake removals are relatively effective in cutting and penetrating soft materials like hides. However, even more importantly, pressure flaking can shape stone flakes in complex and delicate ways that are impossible with other reduction techniques. This is why pressure reduction is used in making projectile points, drills, Early Bronze Age flint daggers, Mayan eccentrics, and other unusual artifact types.

The disadvantages of pressure reduction are similar to those of biface reduction. High-quality raw material is best to work with, special tools are required, and considerable training and specialized skill is necessary to produce most acceptable pieces. Because more vitreous materials are easier to pressure flake, many prehistoric groups that used pressure reduction—and some that used bifacial reduction—developed heat-treating techniques to increase the vitreousness of their raw materials. This consisted of burying roughed-out pieces under a few centimeters of sand and then lighting an intense fire over the spot. This often shifted the colors of raw materials toward the red end of the spectrum and created a shiny luster. These are telltale signs of heat treatment but they do not always occur. In case you are interested in sourcing artifact materials, if heat treatment changes the characteristics of raw materials, they can be difficult to match with untreated source material.

As mentioned at the beginning of this chapter, exactly why pressure-flaked projectile points became so common is an intriguing question since ethnographies document the widespread use of wood, bone, bamboo, and simple flake projectile points on many—if not most—spears and arrows.

Projectile Points for Hunting or Warfare?

Most descriptions of stone projectile points implicitly or explicitly relate their use to hunting, as in fact I often have. However, it needs to be emphasized (following Ellis) that stone projectile points are also overwhelmingly favored for use in warfare. This is undoubtedly because adversaries want to inflict as much lethal and debilitating damage on each other as possible. Even in New Guinea where wood-tipped arrows are used in warfare, the arrow tips are elaborately barbed to create as much pain as possible, and to be as difficult to remove as possible. The barbs are also purposefully undercut to such an extent that they will break off after penetrating a body (Figure 5.13). Similarly, the microlithic barbs on some Mesolithic arrow foreshafts, and the flaring bases of some Neolithic stone arrowheads, seem to be made to break off on penetration into a body.

Before assuming that stone projectile points were mainly used for hunting, therefore, the importance of conflict and warfare should be assessed. Where population densities were relatively high, as in many Neolithic contexts, it is unlikely that many large game animals would have existed in the immediate environment and stone projectile points may have been used in warfare. Stone projectile points are sometimes mainly found around defensive features (e.g., at Hambledon Hill in England), thus also indicating their principal role in warfare.

SUMMARY

In this chapter we examined some of the advantages and disadvantages (the design constraints) of another specialized type of stone tool: projectile points, the iconic tool of stone technology that everyone recognizes but few understand beyond simple platitudes. We then explored the six most common reduction strategies that lithic analysts are likely to encounter when dealing with chipped stone, and tried to understand some of the basic design considerations that seem important in their developments as solutions to practical and prestige problems. There are other less common strategies that exist, such as the African and European Kombewa reduction strategy and undoubtedly others that are particular to specific traditions. These can be explored as needed. It is also useful to consider the production of ground stone cutting tools like adzes as yet another reduction strategy that involves grinding for producing and resharpening edges—a topic to be addressed in Chapter 7.

Having covered the basics of design constraints, possible flake modifications, and basic ways of producing flakes, we are now in a position to examine a few other characteristics that can be inferred from chipped stone tools. To do so, we need to consider additional factors that can be important in the design of stone tools. This is the topic of the next chapter.

Figure 5.13. A wooden barbed arrow from New Guinea used for fighting. It shows the multiple undercut barbs designed to break off on penetrating a body and cause as much damage and pain as possible, as well as being difficult to remove. Many of the Mesolithic composite arrowheads—like the ones in Figure 5.4—may have been designed for the same purpose. In fact, the Australian examples are popularly known as "death spears."

EXERCISE

The goal of this exercise is to make several bipolar cores and obtain flakes from them that are as large and long as possible—ones that might be suitable for skinning a rabbit or even a beaver. In most areas you should be able to find water-rounded pebbles (4–6 centimeters long are usually good). Such pebbles are common either in streambeds or as decorative landscaping around public or private buildings. If these are not available, go to a games store and buy a few of the largest glass marbles you can find. If you have a good source of pebbles, you will want to find ones that flake best and produce the sharpest cutting edges. You may have to try several different types of stone before you find ones that work well, but this is the same thing that people had to do in the past. After you succeed in producing flakes, describe the stone type that worked best. Describe its characteristics: grain size, ease of fracturing, sharpness of edges, how it breaks up (bedding planes or planes of cleavage or homogeneousness), and any other characteristics you think would be important for knapping or using it.

When you have a number of prospective pebble cores, you will next need a stone anvil, perhaps with a depression that can be used to seat your pebble. If no stone anvils are available, concrete surfaces can be used. You will next need a hammerstone. You need to be selective in choosing a hammerstone—one that won't fall apart on impact and one that is heavy enough to initiate a fracture, but not so heavy that you can't hold it securely. In flint knapping a cardinal principle is that flake removal is strongly dependent on the *weight* of the percussor. If you can't get a flake to detach from a core, hitting it harder seldom has much effect. You need a heavier hammerstone. These little pebbles can be surprisingly resistant to fracturing, so you may need to experiment and persist a little.

While bipolar reduction is extremely simple, like using a stone to crack open a nut, the toughness of some stones requires some persistence. If you are holding the pebble upright with your fingers, be careful not to smash your fingers with your hammerstone. Wear gloves or hold the pebble upright with a strip of leather or other material so that your fingers are not in the line of fire. Bash away until the pebble splits and then keep bashing away on the largest piece until you get as many usable flakes as you can. If early hominins could do it with a fraction of your brain size, I'm sure you will be able to succeed as well. Repeat until you have three bipolar cores. What are the edge angles of the bipolar flakes (if you don't have a goniometer/beveled protractor to measure edge angles, estimate them)? How sharp are the flake edges?

Make a simple sketch to scale of one of your bipolar cores. Outline all the edges of flake scars and label all the important features. Include a scale. Describe what the core remnants look like, both at the impact end and the anvil end. Are there any negative bulbs of percussion on the core? Any bulbs of percussion on the flakes? Do you think you could recognize a bipolar core in an assemblage? Bipolar flakes?

ADDITIONAL READINGS

Projectile Points

Ahler, Stanley A. 1971. *Projectile Point Form and Function at Rodgers Shelter, Missouri*. Research Series No. 8, Missouri Archaeological Society, Columbia. This is a key study in establishing the fact that spear points were often part of detachable foreshafts that were used like bifacial knives for butchering after kills were made.

Bradbury, Andrew P. 1997. The Bow and Arrow in the Eastern Woodlands: Evidence for an Archaic Origin. *North American Archaeologist* 18:207–233. There is an extensive literature dealing with when the bow and arrow was introduced into North America, how to distinguish between stone spearheads and arrowheads, the coexistence of both weapons for extended periods, and the advantages and disadvantages of bows over spears. This article is one of the best such discussions and suggests that the use of bows in warfare would have provided some definite advantages.

Ellis, Christopher J. 1997. Factors Influencing the Use of Stone Projectile Tips: An Ethnographic Perspective. In *Projectile Technology*, edited by Heidi Knecht, pp. 37–78. Plenum, New York. The definitive analysis of the use of stone-tipped spears and arrows. It examines factors like the types of game, fighting with stone-tipped weapons, alternative wood- and bone-tipped spears and arrows, and many other factors critical for understanding exactly what stone-tipped projectiles represent and why they were used.

Waguespack, Nicole M., Todd A. Surovell, Allen Denoyer, Alice Dallow, Adam Savage, Jamie Hyneman, and Dan Tapster. 2009. Making a Point: Wood- versus Stone-Tipped Projectiles. *Antiquity* 83:786–800. The authors report the results of experiments measuring the depth of penetration of wood- versus stone-tipped projectiles and found no significant difference (barely 10 percent difference). They conclude that other factors, including social and symbolic considerations, must have been responsible for the adoption of stone-tipped projectiles.

Fracture Mechanics

Lawn, B. R., and D. B. Marshall 1979. Mechanisms of Microcontact Fracture in Brittle Solids. In *Lithic Use-Wear Analysis*, edited by Brian Hayden, pp. 63–82. Academic Press, New York. Understanding that there is a fundamental difference in the fracture mechanics between conchoidal (cone-initiated) fractures and break-initiated fractures (including billet flakes) is essential in lithic analysis—as well as bipolar fractures, which are also distinctive. Lawn and Marshall's chapter explains these differences in terms of fracture mechanics with good, understandable illustrations.

Blade Reduction

Ellis, Christopher J. 2013. Clovis Lithic Technology: The Devil Is in the Details. *Reviews in Anthropology* 42:127–160. This is one of the more cogent discussions of Clovis technology and lifeways that I have seen. Sections on bifacial and blade reduction provide especially good critiques of differing explanations for their adoption.

Gurova, Maria. 2013. Functional Connotations of Large Blades: Examples from Bulgaria. *Revue Archéologique du Centre de la France* Supplement 38:75–84. This article (in French) documents the exceptionally long blades (up to forty centimeters long) produced in Chalcolithic Bulgaria and compares them with similar blades in Iberia. Lack of use and their occurrence in burials indicate their prestige role.

Johnson, Jay K., 1987. Introduction. In *The Organization of Core Technology*, edited by Jay K. Johnson and Carol A. Morrow, pp. 1–21. Westview Press, Boulder, Colorado. This is one of the earliest and clearest propositions that given the weight of stone, mobility has a major effect on the type of reduction adopted—in particular, the development of blade technologies.

Sheets, Payson D., and Guy R. Muto. 1972. Pressure Blades and Total Cutting Edge: An Experiment in Lithic Technology. *Science* 175:632–634. A foundational paper that demonstrates just how much more cutting edge can be obtained from a core used for blade production, as opposed to a core used for simple flake production.

Bipolar Reduction

Hayden, Brian. 1980. Confusion in the Bipolar World: Bashed Pebbles and Splintered Pieces. *Lithic Technology* 9:2–7. This article provides definitions, uses, and distinguishing criteria for bipolar cores versus the lookalike tools called *outils esquillés* or *pièces esquillées*.

Hayden, Brian. 2015. Insights into Early Lithic Technologies from Ethnography. *Philosophical Transactions of the Royal Society B* 370:20140356. This article compares the morphology and metrics of choppers used by Australian Aborigines with those used in the African Oldowan and finds remarkable similarities. It is proposed that they were used for the same types of activities. The argument is also made that the first type of lithic reduction employed at the beginning of the Paleolithic was probably bipolar core reduction for making sharp flakes.

LeBlanc, Raymond. 1992. Wedges, *Pièces Esquillées,* Bipolar Cores, and Other Things: An Alternative to Shott's View of Bipolar Industries. *North American Archaeologist* 13:1–14. LeBlanc makes a strong argument that many bipolar pieces were used as wedges rather than cores.

MacCalman, H. R., and B. J. Grobelaar 1965. Preliminary Report of Two Stone-Working Ova Tjimba Groups in the Northern Kaokoveld of South West Africa. *Cimbebasia* 13:1–39. This is another foundational ethnographic observation of hunter-gatherers expediently using bipolar flake production for the purpose of butchering an animal.

White, J. Peter. 1968. Fabricators, *Outils Ecaillés* or Scalar Cores? *Mankind* 6:171–178. White was one of the pioneers in bringing ethnographic accounts of bipolar flake production to the attention of archaeologists. He amply documents the widespread use of bipolar reduction in the Highlands of New Guinea where he worked, and also describes the lack of intentional retouch on most tools that people made and used.

Bifacial Reduction

Hayden, Brian, and W. Karl Hutchings. 1989. Whither the Billet Flake? In *Experiments in Lithic Technology,* edited by Daniel S. Amick and Raymond P. Mauldin, pp. 235–257. British Archaeological Reports No. 528, Oxford, UK. This is a response to critics who claimed that billet flakes could be produced by hard hammer percussion. It clearly differentiates between hard hammer and soft hammer flakes and describes the criteria that can be used to do so.

Hayden, Brian, and Suzanne Villeneuve. 2009. Sex, Symmetry and Silliness in the Bifacial World. *Antiquity* 83:1163–1175. This is a critique of the suggestion that handaxes were developed by men to attract women.

It explains that bifacial symmetry is simply the best technical approach to maximize the number of flakes from a given mass of raw material and the best way to maintain low edge angles for cutting.

Hester, Thomas R., and W. I. Follett 1976. Yurok Fish Knives: A Study of Wear Patterns and Adhering Salmon Scales. In *Experiment and Function: Four California Studies*, pp. 3–23. Contributions of the Archaeological Research Facility No. 33, University of California, Berkeley. In contrast to the emphasis on developing bifaces for butchering large land mammals, this is an excellent reminder that they can also be developed for butchering large numbers of fish.

Kelly, Robert L. 1988. The Three Sides of a Biface. *American Antiquity* 53:717–734. Kelly takes a similar approach to Johnson's model of blade reduction in his explanation of the use of bifaces in terms of mobility constraints. He also incorporates the availability of lithic raw materials in the equation.

Olausson, Deborah. 1998. Different Strokes for Different Folks: Possible Reasons for Variation in Quality of Knapping. *Lithic Technology* 23:90–110. Olausson makes the important point that people vary considerably in their skill at flint knapping and their ability to learn this craft. She documents this with experimental studies. This is a critical factor in modeling how and why the more complex reduction strategies (including blade and bifacial reduction) developed.

Rust, Horatio N. 1905. The Obsidian Blades of California. *American Anthropologist* 7:688–695. While bifaces may have developed for practical reasons, the technical skill in making them could also be used to create prestige versions, like the Rolls Royce version of the common automobile. In this crtically important article, Rust documents the prestige ritual context and extraordinarily high value of oversized obsidian bifaces among the complex hunter-gatherers of California.

CHAPTER 6

TIER 3:
DESIGN CONSIDERATIONS

Thus far we have concentrated on the mechanics of stone tool manufacture, use, and modification together with basic constraints, design considerations, and design solutions. At the most basic level,
chipped stone is useful for solving problems involving the need to cut
and/or shape wood, bone/antler, meat and skins, and other stones, or
to cut some plants like bamboo, reeds, wheat seed heads, or thatch.
While almost any sharp flake can be used successfully, a second level of
analysis discussed in the last chapter looks at the shape of flakes that
are most suited for specific tasks or contexts and how best to obtain
them from a piece of lithic material.

In this chapter we will look at a third level of design that deals with
what some analysts have called "design considerations," which go beyond
the basic constraints influencing core reduction and flake modification.
These additional considerations include more abstract aspects like reliability, maintainability, versatility, flexibility, diversity, time constraints, and
a few other factors that can affect tool design, manufacturing, and use.

RELIABILITY

Most stone tools are fairly reliable; they don't tend to break up unless
they are unusually thin like billet flakes, microblades, or extremely long,
thin bifaces (which were unlikely to have been practical tools in any
case, but were probably prestige items). Stone projectile points, on the
other hand, tend to break on impact if the target is missed. Thus they are
not very durable or maintainable, or at least not nearly as durable or
maintainable as wood- or bone-tipped spears. However, Peter Bleed

used design theory to propose that some tools seem to be overdesigned for reliability—whether in terms of robustness, carefully fitted parts (and good craftsmanship), or specialist manufacture. Acheulian hand-axes and Oldowan choppers might be considered overdesigned for reliability. Robert Kelly argued that in general bifaces (bifacial knives, or thin bifaces) were reliable tools, a claim that any flintknapper who has fashioned a thin biface might dispute given the frequent breakage when removing billet flakes in the later stages.

It has been suggested that an emphasis on reliability in a given task context probably reflects design constraints in which the consequences of tool failure could be serious. Examples could include spearing a whale from a boat and butchering mass harvests of fish (or bison, or reindeer, or the like). In the case of fish, migrating fish are usually only available for a short period of time—such as a few weeks—during which hundreds or thousands of fish need to be processed and dried for the winter before they spoil. If butchering tools are unreliable, it could mean having to stop butchering fish in order to replace the tool and perhaps travel to a quarry to obtain more stone for tools. This could result in spoilage or loss of fish and hunger in the winter. Robin Torrence emphasized the effects that tight time constraints can have on tool designs, especially where tasks were critical like hunting and mass harvesting.

Thus the design problem is not only how to butcher fish for drying, for instance, but also how to ensure that butchering tools will last for the entire intensive butchering period. There are three obvious design ways to avoid technological breakdowns in food procurement or processing when these are critical activities.

- Make your tools so robust they won't break.
- Stockpile raw material or prefabricated tools to replace broken tools.
- Make tools in a modular fashion so that broken parts can be easily replaced.

Modular tools are often referred to as maintainable tools. Which option is chosen depends a great deal on mobility, transport capabilities, location and nature of lithic raw materials, the absolute quantities to be processed, the time available, the person-power available, special skills required for some of the options, and similar constraints.

MAINTAINABILITY

If completely replacing an entirely dull or broken tool is not practical, there are two basic design solutions to maintain tools that get too dull to use or completely fail: resharpening them or replacing broken or dull parts of composite tools. The number of resharpenings a tool can sustain might be used as one measure of its maintainability; the design of easily replaced component parts is another indicator (e.g., microlithic components of composite tools like slotted antler projectile heads). So Oldowan choppers have low maintainability, Acheulian bifaces have higher maintainability (assuming they were used as tools rather than cores), pressure-flaked bifacial knives are more maintainable, and ground stone cutting implements are even more maintainable (exceeded only by metal cutting tools).

Maintainability is again important in situations where the risk of tool failure creates serious problems, and/or where weight needs to be minimized in transport, and/or where the extent of cutting needs for given periods is considerable. However, simple economy of effort under noncritical situations could conceivably also produce maintainable tools. Conditions of high mobility away from stone tool sources of raw material should also favor maintainable strategies.

The development of microlithic composite tools like single or composite butchering knives (for meat or fish), sickles, and projectile barbs is plausibly related to the strategy of using easily maintainable tools—since microlithic replacement parts are easy to carry around or make as well as replace when broken, while the bone or antler projectile tip is highly resistant to breakage (in contrast to stone points). Microliths can be compared with the snap-off blade segments of zip knives or the throwaway blades in razors. Jelmer Eerkens suggested that Early Mesolithic Europeans primarily used a hunting strategy that relied on carrying around large numbers of microliths prepared in advance of forays featuring intercept hunting. By contrast, he proposed that later Mesolithic strategies produced microliths in smaller batches during encounter hunts. These different strategies produced different patterns archaeologically, with microlithic debitage and cores occurring at residential sites in one case versus at hunting sites in the other case.

VERSATILITY AND MULTIFUNCTIONALITY

Another design consideration (presented by Michael Shott) is tool versatility. Versatility refers to the number of different kinds of tasks in which a tool could be used. It is essentially the same as multifunctionality, a preferable term that seems more descriptive and intuitive. Shott originally thought that versatility could be measured by counting the number of usable edges on a flake; however, this is a very poor measure of different tasks since all edges could be used in the same task event, such as sharpening a wooden or bone spear point or shaping the point of an awl.

On the other hand, one thing that lithic analysts often encounter in assemblages is the occurrence of flakes with two or three kinds of modifications. One edge can have scraper retouch and another edge of the same tool can have a notch or two, but any combination of flake modification techniques is possible: burins and scrapers, expedient knives and notches, intentional breaks and burins, and the like. The recording of multifunctional flakes would be a much better indication of versatility than counting the number of useful edges on flakes. Edges of a single flake with different kinds of use-wear could also be used as indications of multifunctionality. However, any of these measures can be problematic from a conceptual point of view. Of considerable concern is whether the different used parts of the tool were a planned design of the tool or whether they were happenstance, a convenient expedient use of a flake or the recycling of a worn-out tool. It's not clear how this can be determined, but if possible it is probably a good idea to differentiate between tools that were designed to be multifunctional versus those that were simply recycled (like our screwdriver example in Chapter 4).

Bifaces or spurred endscrapers are good examples of tools that were designed for multiple tasks. I suspect that most flakes with multiple edge modifications were not designed for multiple uses but were usually enlisted as scavenged, convenient, expedient solutions to a need for any material that was available and could cut or scrape. In any event, quantifying the proportion of assemblages that are multifunctional should provide some important measures of constraints (such as material availability or mobility), but this should be looked at in terms of specific tools or task sets of tools.

FLEXIBILITY

Michael Shott also proposed using the term "flexibility" to refer to the management of tool forms, a concept that Margaret Nelson attempted to clarify. This is a bit trickier to deal with but would seem to be exemplified by the use of some bifaces described by Robert Kelly and Christopher Ellis.

In this scenario a roughed-out, thick biface would be carried around during seasonal hunting forays and camp movements. Since flakes were needed for sharpening spears or cutting hides or scraping hides, large flakes would be bifacially removed from the roughed-out biface that essentially was used as a core. As the biface became thinner with successive flake removals, its edge would become more serviceable for butchering and sharpening functions and it would be used as a tool, as well as serving as a continuing source of thin flakes for cutting through hides. With yet more continued resharpenings, its size and thinness would become attenuated and it could then be transformed into a spear point like a Clovis point, which—if hafted into a foreshaft—could be easily detached from the main shaft and continue to be used as a butchering knife for kills. If the spear point broke from use, large pieces could still be recycled for the use of broken edges or other edges in sharpening or shaving wooden or bone tools. It is this intended sequential use of successive core/tool designs that seems to be the central concept of flexibility.

Recycled tools might possibly reflect flexible design considerations (e.g., expected final uses as intentional breaks, bipolar cores, and battered pieces/*pièces écaillées*); however, it is difficult to know to what extent this recycling was an intended design aspect of the tool versus simple expedient scavenging. Similarly, as mentioned before, when there are two or more types of edge modification on a multifunctional flake, it is difficult to tell if they constitute sequential recycling of the flake or if they were employed at the same event for different aspects of a single task. Thus there are a number of problems involved in trying to operationalize some of these conceptual distinctions, and it might be more meaningful to find a way to combine measures of multifunctionality and flexibility into a single concept and measure. Alternatively, they could just be labeled as clear instances of recycling or multifunctional use of flakes.

DIVERSITY

Michael Shott also demonstrated the strong influence that mobility constraints have on the diversity of tool types in assemblages. It makes sense that the more one moves around, the more one needs to reduce the amount of things carried, so people try to make their stone tool assemblage multifunctional and their reduction strategies flexible (Figure 6.1). Carrying around stone raw material, after all, is taxing on the body and one can use a fair amount of stone over the course of a season. By contrast, the more sedentary one is, the more stuff one can accumulate so that people can keep and maintain more specialized types of tools. In addition, more sedentary lifestyles are usually associated with the mass harvesting and processing of seasonal resources, and—as explained in Chapter 2—mass processing generally leads to increased specialization and increased numbers of tool types.

Robin Torrence applied this same logic to the complexity of tools. While these suggestions make good theoretical sense, in any attempt to quantify diversity, there will be the thorny issue of what constitutes individual type categories that are being used to measure diversity. Should scrapers be divided into ten or more categories according to edge shapes, orientations, and normal or inverse retouch—as François Bordes did for the Mousterian? Or should all these variants be collapsed into a single functional scraper type—as Harold Dibble argued for the Mousterian? Should multifunctional tools be counted as a separate type for

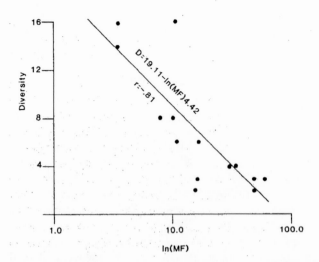

Figure 6.1. In order to demonstrate the effect of mobility on the diversity of tools, Michael Shott graphed the number of types of tools ethnographically recorded for various groups against the frequency of their moves in annual rounds. The result is a very convincing relationship showing that as mobility frequency (MF) increases, the number of tool types is reduced. Presumably, this would apply to stone tools as well as all the tools (wood, bone, antler, metal) used in Shott's analysis. (From Shott 1986, p. 25, Figure 3)

each kind of edge modification present (i.e., a flake with both scraper and notch retouch counted as two tools)? Should only the last use be counted (where it can even be determined)? Or should a separate type be created for each combination of different tool modifications? What about types that not all analysts recognize such as intentional breaks, notches, bipolar cores, and expedient knives? What are the most meaningful criteria that should be used to classify tools for diversity or other measures? These kinds of issues are difficult to resolve.

OTHER DESIGN CONSIDERATIONS

Similar to his distinction between situational versus personal gear, Lewis Binford proposed that expedient (short-lived) tools have different design strategies from curated (long-lived) tools. This is undoubtedly reflected in the degree of resharpening, specialized manufacture, and selection of raw materials—among other design considerations. He also suggested differentiating between extractive versus processing types of tools, which makes good sense in terms of trying to model the tasks of a community (e.g., projectile points for killing versus butchering, or tanning tools for processing, or sickles for harvesting wheat, versus grinding stones for processing grains).

In considering such issues, I would like to iterate the very substantial importance of the quantity of material being processed in designing tools. Other design-related considerations may be proposed in the future as well, but at this point most of the basics are in hand for a fairly comprehensive understanding of lithic technologies, their constraints, and why they changed over time. It remains to apply them in a holistic manner.

COMMENTARY

Aside from a number of difficulties in operationalizing some of the above concepts (which Nora Franco, Jim Spafford, and I discussed), a number of analysts have attempted to characterize entire assemblages as structured around maintainability, reliability, flexibility, or other similar concepts. From my perspective this is a very coarse-grained approach to lithic analysis that may provide some useful comparative information, but which combines so many disparate dimensions of lithic use that the results must often be of questionable worth.

Such global characterizations of assemblages combine carefully crafted tools made of fine exotic materials with expediently made tools of inferior local materials; they combine tasks having specific tool needs like quartzite spall scrapers with utilized flakes with many possible uses; and they combine tools designed for use at residential sites with tools designed for procurement forays like hunting. In short, entire assemblage characterizations include so many different design strategies that the results lack much meaning—sort of like a nutritionist who only assessed diets in terms of the amount of "food" or "calories" instead of looking at the contributions of meat, starches, vegetables, lipids, sugars, and vitamins/minerals in a person's diet. In fact, I am hard pressed to think of any lithic analyses that have quantified assemblages in terms of the concepts proposed above. And even when applied to a single tool type like bifaces, analysts like Paul Ewonus have questioned the usefulness of these concepts in terms of explaining tool designs.

Identifying Tasks and Strategies

In lithics it would be much more informative to use reliability, maintainability, multifunctionality, flexibility, or other design aspects to characterize specific task-related tools. It is worth iterating that assemblages are composed of different types of strategies for dealing with different problems, and it makes most sense to identify the different strategies represented in assemblages and analyze tools in those terms. Hence it is necessary to "deconstruct" assemblages into their component task sets. This basic notion may be recognized by some analysts in dealing with hunting tools like projectile points, but it rarely goes beyond this—except where ground stone might be concerned.

It is important to recognize there is no single constraint that explains all the variations in stone tool assemblages, and there is no single measure of assemblages that reflects all strategies. For some purposes and constraints, local low-quality coarse-grained materials may constitute optimal design uses; for other purposes with other constraints, higher-quality materials provide optimal design uses. For some strategies the production of blades might be most suitable; for other strategies a simple flake is all that is needed. One goal of lithic research should be to understand why low-grade local materials versus high-grade exotics were used, or why a given reduction strategy was used.

In order to understand stone tools, it becomes critical to isolate the different strategies that comprise assemblages rather than combine artifacts from different strategies. Two excellent examples of this are Jeffrey Flenniken's study of microflake uses for butchering salmon at the Hoko River site and Michael Rousseau's analysis of distinctive "key-shaped" scrapers on the Northwest Plateaux of North America. In contrast to Flenniken's analysis focused on a specific task and related tool types, many analysts blend and blur different strategies in dealing with categories like formed and unformed tools, bipolar items, or bifaces (defined by many analysts as anything with bifacial retouch). The result of such categories are artifact counts and statistics that no one can explain. On the other hand, some concepts like measures of tool diversity in assemblages (i.e., the total number of different tool types in assemblages) can only be meaningfully applied to entire assemblages—although what constitutes individual types needs to be carefully thought out.

TYPES

Since I raised the issue of how the construction of typologies can affect attempts to compare the diversity of tool types between assemblages, a word or two more about typologies seems warranted, but the topic can be daunting. As Gordon Willey was once reported to have said, "Typology is long and life is fleeting." Therefore we won't go into typology in much detail except to discuss the usefulness and goals of typologies.

If you undertake an analysis of stone tools, you will need to use a typology of some sort. What kind of a typology are you going to use? In one of the more lucid treatments of the topic, James Hill and Robert Evans pointed out that typologies are created in order to deal with specific problems. If you are doing an analysis for a consulting company or a government agency, the typology may already be decided for you—in which case you choose the typology that will solve the problem of submitting an acceptable report. These companies and agencies usually want archaeologists to use a typology that will make it possible to document sites in comparable ways to solve administrative and accountability problems. Questions of technological or social organization are frequently irrelevant to these concerns.

On the other hand, if an academic researcher who has excavated a site wants you to analyze his or her lithic assemblage, the first thing that you need to ask is "What do they want to find out from their lithics?" The answer should determine every other step in your analysis, although you could add other things that you have a personal interest in or that you think other researchers would want to know about.

Traditional Typologies

This may be an overly idealistic expectation. In many or most regions, there already exists an accepted standard typology for analyzing stone tools. If you opt to use that typology, it will simply be to solve the problem of getting the analysis done without asking other questions.

How did these standard typologies come to exist? My view is that they are held over from the very long period of archaeological development from 1836—when Christian Thomson published his thesis on the Stone Age of technological evolution—until 1949, when Gordon Libby found a way of dating archaeological deposits using carbon isotopes. During this formative century of archaeology, the biggest problem confronting archaeologists was determining how old their artifacts were and what cultures they belonged to. Almost all archaeological energy was consumed in trying to answer these questions.

One of the major techniques developed for determining the age of archaeological remains was to construct typologies of artifacts that were time and culture sensitive. This approach was derived from the geological use of different types of fossils to identify different geological time periods, and in fact some stone tool types were referred to as *fossiles directeurs*. Thus handaxes were diagnostic of the early Paleolithic (literally the "Old Stone Age"); blades, burins, thin bifaces, and certain styles of projectile points were typical of the later Stone Age; and ground stone celts indicated the New Stone Age. Specific styles and innovations became associated with specific archaeological cultures. These typologies were refined over time with statistical accounts of proportional frequencies of retouched tools that were thought to change in popularity according to time and place, but the basic types became fixed.

Contemporary Typologies

It was only when dating deposits became easy and accurate—by using radioactive isotopes or similar techniques—that archaeological resources, time, and energy could turn to other questions that required different types of types to deal with. Enter Hill and Evans who pointed out the long-forgotten logic of creating types. Today, if we want to know what tools were used for, we have types of use-wear, types of residues, types of resharpening, types of prehension or hafting, utilitarian types and prestige types, and other types. If we want to know about exchanges and interactions between groups, we have stylistic types that are particular to each group and stone material types that are found only in different group territories. If we want to know about socioeconomic inequalities, we develop types that reflect the investment costs in the procurement of materials, the manufacture of items, and the production of tools like endscrapers for making prestige items, or drills for making beads.

How to go about creating such typologies can be subjective and simple (but difficult to justify or reproduce) or it can be objective and complex (but explicitly justified and reproducible). If you are asked to undertake a lithic analysis, these and other choices will mainly be up to you.

EXERCISE

List as many separate task sets that you can think of for a simple hunter-gatherer group that would have existed in your geographical area. Include all the types of stone tools that might be included in each. If there were more complex, sedentary hunter-gatherers in your area, do the same for them.

ADDITIONAL READINGS

Bleed, Peter. 1986. The Optimal Design of Hunting Weapons: Maintainability or Reliability? *American Antiquity* 51:737–747. This is another foundational article that introduced and elaborated design considerations in lithic analysis to include maintainable and reliability features of tools.

Eerkens, Jelmer W. 1998. Reliable and Maintainable Technologies: Artifact Standardization and the Early to Later Mesolithic Transition in Northern England. *Lithic Technology* 23:42–53. One of the better attempts to use reliability and maintainability design features to explain changes in microlithic technology during the Mesolithic.

Ewonus, Paul. 2009. Design Theory Analysis of Biface Technology. *Canadian Student Journal of Anthropology* 21:83–101. This is one of the few comprehensive attempts to apply design theory analysis to a specific tool type. While most conclusions might be predictable, Ewonus found that the concepts of reliability, maintainability, or other design considerations did not contribute to understanding the design of bifaces on the Northwest Plateau.

Hill, James N., and Robert K. Evans 1972. A Model for Classification and Typology. In *Models in Archaeology*, edited by David L. Clarke, pp. 231–273. Methuen, London. In contrast to the then prevailing approach of using "received" typologies, Hill and Evans argue for the development and use of a range of typologies developed to deal with specific problems.

Nelson, Margaret. 1991. The Study of Technological Organization. *Archaeological Method and Theory* 3:57–100. This is an example of the proposed use of global characteristics of lithic assemblages to help understand overall technological organization—including assessments of maintainability, reliability, diversity, versatility, and others.

Shott, Michael J. 1986. Technological Organization and Settlement Mobility: An Ethnographic Examination. *Journal of Anthropological Research* 42:15–51. In this article Shott clearly shows how mobility affects the diversity of tools in given technologies with an impressive use of graphed ethnographic data (see Figure 6.1). He also discusses the concepts of versatility and flexibility.

Torrence, Robin. 1983. Time Budgeting and Hunter-Gatherer Technology. In *Hunter-Gatherer Economy in Prehistory: A European Perspective*, edited by Geoff Bailey, pp. 11–22. Cambridge University Press, Cambridge, UK. Torrence was the main person to have drawn attention to the time constraints that could affect tool design in some hunter-gatherer tasks like butchering. This is her key publication on the topic.

CHAPTER 7

CHANGES

In the following discussion, we want to look at one particular aspect of tool design—resharpening. The type of stone material used or suitable for various resharpening strategies varies, so before delving into resharpening, I would like to digress briefly to examine how materials should be incorporated into design considerations.Since it was the makers of stone tools who made the decisions, we should logically adopt their perspective rather than using typologies of industrial geologists. We cannot know for sure how people of the distant past may have conceived of stones or categorized them. Nevertheless, these people consistently chose stones with certain characteristics for various tasks and materials that were probably recognized as different types of stones. What were the characteristics they used to choose materials for making stone tools?

RAW MATERIALS

To begin, we need to recognize that the best material for a wide range of tasks is not always flint or chert or obsidian, and that in any event these are industrial, science-based types, not indigenous ones. The earliest Oldowan choppers were made of fine crystalline basalts, as were similar chopper tools that I observed being used to shape grinding stones in Guatemala. Interestingly, obsidian is widely preferred by contemporary flintknappers for making beautiful pressure-flaked knives and projectile points due to its ease of pressure flaking. With the sharpest edges that can be attained by any material, obsidian is extremely good for cutting operations like scarifications at initiations, and it was often valued as a prestige material.

Should we think poorly of the Oldowans who did not have access to obsidian? No. They had other, relatively more vitreous materials that they also used. They chose the grainier basalt because they wanted to. Obsidian is one of the most brittle and breakable stone materials and thus was usually avoided for tasks involving impacts or high-contact energies because it would shatter on impact. For doing some tasks, coarser-grained materials are often preferred due to their resistance to edge fracturing in high-impact energy situations like chopping into wood.

Initially, what prehistoric people would have wanted to know is the same thing you probably wanted to know in the exercise in Chapter 1. What kinds of rocks are capable of having sharp edges, sharp enough to cut into wood or even antler or bone? These kinds of stones are overwhelmingly characterized by their ability to fracture in a conchoidal fashion. There may be occasional other rocks like slate that can split to create sharp edges, but they are usually fairly fragile edges, and this is another consideration (i.e., the brittleness or fragility of the edges). Oldowans and others needed edges that would stand up to some heavy use. As it turns out, there is a range of rock types—some stronger than others—that can support good cutting edges: flints (including cherts), chalcedonies, rhyolites, dacites, andesites, basalts, vitrified tuffs, quartzites or other silicified sedimentary rocks, natural glasses (obsidian, crystal quartz), and undoubtedly more.

It's doubtful that all these scientific types of stone would have had separate terms prehistorically. They may have all been lumped into one linguistic taxon, or some of the especially striking types like quartz crystal and obsidian may have been recognized as special rock types, or they may have been differentiated by color. But the essential thing was that they were viewed as good tool stones with useful mechanical qualities.

Geological Nomenclature versus Prehistoric Choices

Sometimes the scientific or geological description of material actually masks the characteristics of most importance to the prehistoric users of stone and archaeologists. Geologically, chert is an amazingly varied type of rock and includes many geological specimens that archaeologists would probably not even recognize as chert. The cherts used prehistorically were often of relatively pure silica, but a range of geological cherts could also be used that had varying levels of impurities—like clays or silts that can sometimes be so abundant that these cherts have a grainy texture more like siltstone or mudstone. Fracture and edges might still be usable, but are not as strong as the purer silica varieties of chert and may not be as suitable for use-wear analysis or fine pressure flaking.

Thus simply describing materials as flint or chert or any other geological type developed for industrial purposes really does not convey what was most important to stone tool makers of the past. It would be much more useful to describe the brittleness or toughness of cutting edges, grain sizes of the matrix, the type of fracture, the purity of silica, the sharpness of given edge angles, the ease of flaking, the shape of raw material, and other material characteristics specific to the stones that were actually used by prehistoric technologists. Obviously, there was also variation in the types of stones chosen in the past—even for a specific task. Assessing the full range represented in given tool types, together with the most common characteristics of interest to users, would be an ideal way to analyze stone materials. However, the practicality of doing this given current funding priorities has yet to be successfully addressed.

Interestingly, when I did ethnoarchaeology with Australian Aboriginals involving stone tool manufacturing and use, women were prohibited from using any cryptocrystalline materials. Only men could use these purer and more visually attractive stones. Women had to use coarser quartzites or other non-cyptocrysalline rocks. Earlier Australian ethnographers in other parts of the continent reported the same prohibition.

RESHARPENING STRATEGIES OVER TIME

One of the main things I have tried to stress in understanding stone tool design and use is the importance of the magnitude of demands for cutting tools in relation to the availability of—or ease of procurement of—suitable stone materials. Time and transport constraints in the procurement of stone, as well as the nature of the materials to be cut, are also critical factors. There are a number of ways to evaluate the need versus availability of stone materials. The tool : debitage ratio should reflect the relative abundance of stone material or the scarcity thereof. The amount of recycling of stone materials (broken tools further reduced by bipolar reduction or intentional breakage to use right angle edges), or the proportion of multifunctional tools in the total tool assemblage, provide proxy measures of shortages in raw materials. The relative importance of curated tools (end scrapers, bifaces, drills, or other tools) might also be used as an indicator.

In addition, reduction strategies that maximized the amount of cutting edge produced per unit of weight of raw material should be a major indicator of past increases in demands and availability of raw materials—since reduction strategies like blade reduction, bifacial reduction, pressure reduction, and bipolar reduction primarily make sense in terms of an increased demand for more and more renewable cutting edges.

The average size of tools should also indicate the availability of raw material. Not only tools, but debitage that is specific to particular reduction strategies, can indicate the relative importance of types of reduction strategies represented in assemblages. Michael Shott and Mark Seeman have evaluated several different ways of calculating the amount of material removed from flakes due to resharpenings. One would expect more resharpenings under conditions of increased demand for cutting tools.

A brief overview of the changes in resharpening strategies over time can help illustrate some of these concepts, beginning with the Oldowan.

The Oldowan

About two million years ago, our ancestors began fashioning choppers from basalt cobbles that they carried around the landscape for distances of ten kilometers or more. What were they doing with these tools?

On the basis of my ethnoarchaeological work with Australian Aboriginals, there are good reasons to think that the choppers were used for woodworking—probably cutting and sharpening saplings for spears, throwing sticks, digging sticks, or shelters. From what we can tell about subsistence in Oldowan times, it seems that hunting had been adopted but it is unlikely that hunting was perfected to a proficient degree or was very significant in Oldowan diets. Scavenging kills from other predators, or perhaps driving predators from their kills with rocks and spears, were probably more widely used. Therefore the need for replacing or resharpening spears or cutting through the skin of animals was probably limited. A few spears and digging sticks used occasionally in the course of a month could be adequately made and maintained by carrying around one chopper and a small number of flakes used only a few times. Cutting through animal skin to access meat could have been dealt with efficiently by carrying around coarse-grained flakes from choppers or finer-grained flakes from elsewhere, or by flaking quartz pebbles in the environment using bipolar reduction.

At this point it should be remembered that choppers were made using hard hammer percussors (i.e., hammerstones) and that hard hammer reduction of grainy materials like basalt removes large areas of the striking platforms, as you will discover if you start flint knapping yourself. The flakes, especially in grainy materials, are also frequently rather short. The result is that few flakes can be removed from a block of stone and the edge angles tend to rapidly increase as successive flakes are removed (see Figure 5.7). Therefore choppers have limited use-lives in terms of total active use-time.

If you only need to use a chopper occasionally, and can be assured of being able to obtain another block of raw material before your old one is exhausted, then the short active use-time is not a concern—especially if choppers can be shared within a band of hunter-gatherers. A limited amount of material needing to be processed means that minimal effort can be spent in procuring and making tools, similar to the solutions for opening a single bottle of beer or cutting down a single young tree.

Acheulian Handaxes and Mousterian Levallois Flakes

What happens, then, when hunters become more proficient and start bringing down game more frequently? As explained in Chapter 5, the need for replacing and resharpening spears increases, as does the demand for stone materials suitable for cutting through animal hides and butchering. At a critical point, stone becomes too onerous to acquire and carry around using hard hammer reduction and other ways have to be found to extend the active use-lives of tools. Otherwise the frequency of hunting and kills has to be curtailed or reduced. The adoption of bifacial reduction and the Acheulian handaxe was a common design solution under these circumstances. However, the handaxe came at a cost. It required better materials and more skill and training to make, as well as a need to carry around specialized billets for removing flakes.

The production of Levallois flakes can be considered an offshoot of the development of Acheulian bifaces since the reduction procedures are essentially identical. Moreover, Levallois flakes began appearing in the Late Acheulian and continued through much of the Middle Paleolithic, perhaps partially replacing the need for Acheulian bifaces as a source of sharp skinning flakes—since Levallois flakes had cutting edges around their entire perimeter. However, much more research needs to be done to fully explain the widespread abandonment of handaxe technology in the Middle Paleolithic.

The bifacial handaxe was adopted throughout most of Africa and Europe and much of Asia. Interestingly, its adoption stopped just east of India and choppers continued to be used throughout the rest of Asia until the end of the Paleolithic, when ground stone cutting tools were adopted. The geographical limit of handaxe occurrence is sometimes called the "Movius Line" after Harvard University archaeologist Hallam Movius, who brought this curious distribution to the attention of scholars.

Why bifacial reduction was never adopted east of the Movius Line has always intrigued prehistorians. From a design perspective, the explanation should be that (a) hunting did not take place frequently enough to warrant the extra investments required for bifacial reduction, or (b) other solutions were found to fulfill the cutting requirements of the time. Specifically, it has been suggested that split bamboo—which has very sharp edges—could be used as knives for skinning and butchering, since bamboo contains high amounts of silica and such bamboo knives were used ethnographically for cutting meat or other things. Given the rapid diffusion of other technological innovations (such as the bows and arrow, microlithic technology, stone boiling, fishing technology, ground stone technology, pottery, and domesticated species) across the globe, the argument that people in the Far East were unaware of bifacial technology and that no one thought of it is simply not credible.

Upper Paleolithic Blades and Bifaces

While Neandertals may have occasionally aggregated and had enough hunters to bring down one or more large nasty ungulates like aurochs or bison (e.g., at sites like Coudoulous and Mauran in France), most of the time they appear to have lived in small bands of 12–25 people with 2–5 active hunters who only used hand-thrown spears—a technology similar to that used by the ethnographic Tasmanians. When briefly aggregated into groups five or ten times this size (60–250 people), they could probably consume most of the meat from large kills over the span of a week or two. Some of the meat may even have been dried for later use, although the quantity was probably small, requiring no specialized filleting tools.

Enter *Homo sapiens sapiens*, Anatomically Modern Hominins with an Upper Paleolithic technology not only for killing large numbers of animals (spearthrowers and nets), but also for preserving and storing large amounts of meat from mass kills. Meat storage enabled them to live in larger, more numerous groups so that the population increased exponentially during the Upper Paleolithic. Larger groups also meant more people and more hunters who could be used in game drives for seasonal mass kills and regular kills throughout the rest of the year. The ability to live in groups that were probably five or more times larger than Neandertal bands must have given Upper Paleolithic groups critical advantages in any conflicts over resources or land. The expansion into Neandertal territories was therefore relentless—just as relentless as the spread of Europeans with metal industrial technology into the tribal areas of the world where stone technology was still used.

Irrespective of the consequences, there must have been a strong need to process large amounts of meat from mass kills (up to five hundred antelope in one event in Near Eastern ethnographic accounts, as well as similar amounts of meat inferred from archaeological analyses or kills of very large animals). The meat from these kills had to be dried for storage before spoilage occurred. This would have created significant constraints on the time available to process very large amounts of meat, thus increasing the need to extract yet larger amounts of cutting edge that could be derived from a block of stone. In addition, as Rob

Gargett and I have shown, the greater the processing volumes, the more specialized and task-specific tools become, resulting in more types of tools for a given task (see Chapter 2). Specialized blade technology and bi-facial reduction—particularly in some cases like thin bifacial knives—make very good sense in this context from a design perspective (see Chapter 4).

One aspect of the Upper Paleolithic—and many Middle Paleolithic and Mesolithic—assemblages that has always puzzled me is what tools were used for cutting the saplings needed for spears, digging sticks, and shelters. There are very occasional chopper-like tools in some assemblages, but not the number that one would expect from such recurring need. Perhaps the stones and tools used for such purposes were expediently made and discarded at the procurement sites (as I have documented in Australia), or perhaps cores were used initially for such tasks and then further reduced for flakes, but it still seems surprising that there are not more identifiable heavy-duty woodworking chipped stone tools in these assemblages.

Mesolithic Microliths

Even further increases in obtaining cutting edges from given sizes or weights of stone materials were developed with the reduction of flake or blade sizes to microlithic proportions and the introduction of pressure flaking—characteristics that originally were thought to define the Mesolithic as a transitional technology between the Old Stone Age hard hammer and billet-based technology and the New Stone Age technology using ground stone cutting tools. However, both microliths and pressure flaking actually began earlier in the Upper Paleolithic of Europe and the Far East and southern Africa, perhaps in response to the spread of forests and the more frequent use of pursuit hunting rather than mass kills. But both microliths and pressure flaking eventually became much more widespread elsewhere in the Mesolithic/Epipaleolithic/Archaic world, and these technologies are still often depicted as associated with Pene-Pleistocene or Holocene cultures.

Ground Stone Axes

At one time considered the hallmark of the New Stone Age, ground stone axes similarly first appeared in the Mesolithic of Europe and the late Pleistocene of the Far East. They also occurred in North America among many late Archaic types of cultures. Was the appearance of ground-edge technology due to brilliant discoveries, or was it a commonsense development stemming from a change in design constraints? I was convinced that it was not the result of a brilliant discovery when my five-year-old son, who had seen me use flakes of obsidian, began playing with other pieces of stone and ground the edge of one stone into something resembling a cutting edge, then proudly showed it to me. I thought that if a five-year-old could come up with such an innovation in technology, then *Homo habilis* or *Homo erectus* probably could have done the same if they had thought it was advantageous to do so several million years ago.

So what are the design advantages and disadvantages of ground stone cutting tools, and how could the constraints have changed to make them more attractive to use than simple flaked choppers? Essentially, what really characterized the Mesolithic—and perhaps the Late Pleistocene cultures in some areas—was a number of new technologies that enabled people to extract resources from different kinds of environments. This resulted in greater degrees of sedentism in richer resource areas, although high mobility persisted in poorer areas.

Some of these new technologies and settlements required cutting wood on a far grander scale than had hitherto been necessary. In particular, the construction of weirs with hundreds of wood stakes, the construction of dugout or frame canoes or boats, and the construction of more permanent shelters all required a substantial amount of woodcutting. Undertaking these tasks with handheld chipped stone choppers would not only result in a lot of hand trauma, but would also require a huge amount of stone raw material to replace exhausted choppers or bifaces. The main advantage of ground stone cutting tools is that their edges are more resistant to use chipping and last much longer than chipped stone cutting tools. In addition, by using grinding techniques, workers can get many more resharpenings from a piece of stone than they can from billet flaking.

Nor could pressure flaking of large heavy cutting tools maintain an appropriate edge for long. Resharpening by using pressure flaking is really only effective on knife-sized materials. The disadvantages of using ground stone cutting tools are threefold.

- They involve specific kinds of stone materials that require special trips to obtain.
- They require special skills to quarry, rough out, and grind to shape.
- They require good grinding (wet) stones and considerable time and effort to fashion and resharpen.

However, as with billet flaking and pressure flaking, increased investment in tool manufacturing and maintenance seems to have been worthwhile given the need to process large volumes of materials. The considerable time and effort needed to manufacture the best ground stone axes also made them useful for prestige displays. And their use in warfare should also not be overlooked.

This finishes my short odyssey into the evolution of resharpening techniques. This analysis of resharpening techniques could also be extended into the Chalcolithic and Bronze ages in order to account for the adoption of even more costly tools for cutting—ones made out of metal that were more effective and could be resharpened even more times. However, further consideration of the adoption of metals would go well beyond the immediate scope of understanding chipped stone tools.

ADDITIONAL READINGS

Darwent, John. 1998. *The Prehistoric Use of Nephrite on the British Columbia Plateau.* Archaeology Press, Simon Fraser University, Burnaby, British Columbia, Canada. This is an excellent study of the costs and benefits of making and using nephrite ground stone adzes. Darwent made a nephrite adze using traditional techniques, spending over a hundred hours to do so. Given such a cost, one has to wonder what benefits could have warranted the manufacture of such adzes.

Hayden, Brian. 1989. From Chopper to Celt: The Evolution of Resharpening Techniques. In *Time, Energy and Stone Tools*, edited by Robin Torrence, pp. 7–16. Cambridge University Press, Cambridge, UK. The publication on which most of this chapter is based. It provides greater detail for the model.

Hayden, Brian. 2012. Neandertal Social Structure? *Oxford Journal of Archaeology* 31:1–26. The views of Neandertal band sizes, aggregation groups, frequencies of large mammal kills, territorial sizes, and transport of raw materials over the landscape are presented in this article.

Legge, A. J., and P. A. Rowley-Conwy. 2000. The Exploitation of Animals. In *Village on the Euphrates: From Foraging to Farming at Abu Hureyra*, edited by A. M. T. Moore, G. C. Hillman, and A. J. Legge, pp. 424–471. Oxford University Press, London. The main value of this study of archaeological fauna is the ethnographic and archaeological evidence of mass kills of antelope, attaining up to five hundred animals killed in single events. This provides some idea of the constraints that people using stone butchering tools would have faced in the past.

Pétrequin, Pierre, and Pétrequin, Anne-Marie. 1993. *Ecologie d'un outil: La hache de pierre en Irian Jaya (Indonésie)*. Monograph du CRA 12. CNRS

Editions, Paris. Together with O. W. Hampton's book *Culture of Stone* (1999), this work provides the definitive study of ground edge axes and adzes in New Guinea. Both books are ethnographic treasures.

Shott, Michael, and Mark Seeman 2017. Use and Multifactorial Reconciliation of Uniface Reduction Measures: A Pilot Study at the Nobles Pond Paleoindian Site. *American Antiquity* 82:723–741. This article proposes a fairly complicated—but seemingly very accurate—technique for estimating the amount of edge that has been removed from a flake by successive resharpenings. Ultimately, aside from subjective estimates, it may be the only way of quantifying this kind of information.

CHAPTER 8

TOTAL ASSEMBLAGES

Having delved into design approaches to understanding chipped stone tools, and discussed how to analyze the most common kinds of tools and reduction strategies, it is time to see how all this might fit together in the analysis of an actual assemblage. I will use an abbreviated version of my analysis of the assemblage from the Keatley Creek site in the Interior Plateau of British Columbia, a seasonally sedentary occupation with over one hundred housepit structures occupied approximately 1,000–2,000 years ago or more (Figure 8.1). There are a number of initial observations we can make in terms of the design problems that members of this community would have solved with lithic solutions, as well as the constraints they had to work with in developing these solutions.

PROFILE OF THE KEATLEY CREEK SITE

The main staple and source of wealth for residents at Keatley Creek were the abundant salmon runs that seasonally choked the Fraser River near the site for a month or two. Every year each family caught, filleted, dried, and stored hundreds or thousands of migrating salmon during the intensive fish runs in the nearby Fraser River. Stored food largely made possible the seasonally sedentary housepit occupations from October or November to March. People traveled into the mountains in the summer, when both game and edible roots were relatively abundant, and then moved to fishing camps along the river in the fall. Hunting and plant-collecting forays could happen at other times throughout the year, although less frequently during the busy fishing season and in the winter.

121

Like other hunter-gatherers in temperate climates, the residents of Keatley Creek faced the basic problems of how to capture and process game and/or fish, how to obtain plant foods, how to stay warm in cold winters, and how to create shelter. In addition, we view the occupants as complex hunter-gatherers who formed corporate groups that owned fishing and hunting/root-gathering areas, hosted feasts, and used a number of prestige goods in order to solve sociopolitical problems such as creating alliances, acquiring political dominance, and obtaining access to resources via selective marriages. These prestige goods included shells from the coast hundreds of kilometers away; obsidian from far to the north and south; and locally sourced copper, soapstone, and nephrite for adzes. The major constraints they had to deal with were the type, quantity, and seasonality of food and other available resources (including stone), mobility patterns, transport capabilities, and the population of the community.

Some specialized tools could be specific to seasonally occupied sites. For instance, tools used for butchering and filleting fish would only be expected to occur at fishing camps. There would be no reason for them to occur in the mountains or at winter villages unless some of the tools were multifunctional, such as bifacial knives and bifacial thinning flakes that could be used for butchering fish as well as hunted animals. By contrast, tools used to make birch bark baskets would probably only occur at housepit villages located near the streams where birch trees occurred. Although most deer hides were obtained in the mountains, many of them were probably worked at the village sites when there was more time to undertake this laborious process.

The Lithic Assemblage at Keatley Creek

Vitreous, cryptocrystalline, and fine-grained types of trachydacite—as well as yellow-brown chert raw materials—were the main stone types

Figure 8.1. This panoramic view of the Keatley Creek site shows the core of the village with pithouse depressions clearly visible. A number of interesting outlier structures occur to the left on the other side of the creek. Photo by Suzanne Villeneuve.

used for chipped stone, although several other cryptocrystalline silicates were sometimes used for which the sources are unknown. With very few exceptions, 90 percent or more of all debitage and tools at housepits were made of the black trachydacites. They came mainly from the nearby mountain valleys located at least ten kilometers away, and almost all the lithic materials needed over the winter were presumably collected during the summer hunts in the mountains and brought to the winter housepit villages carried by individuals or dogs (at least one of the Keatley Creek dogs had deformed vertebrae from carrying heavy packs).

It should be remembered that people returning from the mountains to the winter villages would have had considerable transport constraints. They would have had to carry harvested and dried roots, dried meat, dried deer hides, antlers, spears or bows and arrows, throwing sticks, babies, an array of non-lithic tools (billets, fire-making kits, cordage, baskets), and perhaps extra clothes or robes for inclement and cold weather (it could snow in the mountains any month of the year) or even sheltering materials like mats. It is also important to note that travel to mountain sources to restock core materials would not be feasible in the winter—besides which all the quarry areas, streams, and ground would be frozen solid by winter temperatures that usually were –20 degrees or colder.

Thus no replenishment of raw materials was generally possible during the winter and there would have been major constraints on how much stone would be available during the occupation of the winter village. However, coarse-grained quartzite cobbles could be found along the streams and in cutbanks along the Fraser River, but do not seem to have been as effective as trachydacites for most tasks; in fact, quartzites were almost exclusively used as spalls for scraping hides. Supplies of the finer cryptocrystalline materials could be augmented by trade, but judging from the low percentage of exotic lithic materials at the site, this does not appear to have been very important.

Some accounts of winter life in pithouses characterized it as not very active. It has even been described to me as being like hibernation, giving the impression of a lot of sleeping and not too many activities that would demand the use of stone tools—aside from some meal preparations and making display materials for occasional feasts. Despite such views, there is a fair amount of lithic debitage associated with housepit floors and middens, indicating that some gear manufacturing and maintenance or other activities were clearly taking place on a routine basis. In light of the above constraints, how was stone for tools managed and used at this winter village site?

The Block Core Strategy

Block cores were the dominant reduction strategy used at Keatley Creek. They seem to have been stored in the pithouses and expediently retrieved when needed to obtain one or more suitable flakes, which were then discarded after use unless they had unusual characteristics. Most flake debitage and tools from block cores were 2–3 centimeters in length, indicating fairly small and light tasks. Most tools exhibited relatively minimal degrees of resharpening.

All these characteristics make sense from a design perspective in terms of varied, episodic, light tasks involving the removal of small amounts of wood or bone/antler material from the items being worked. Thus there was no need to fashion specific formal flake types like blades or Levallois flakes from block cores, just flakes that could and would perform the light tasks at hand. Simple flakes from block cores are extremely versatile. According to Jim Spafford's analysis, about a third to a fifth of the tools from housepits were small, utilized flakes, almost all from block cores. They could have been used in a wide range of tasks—from smoothing or sharpening spears and arrows or spearthrowers and bows to thinning basket elements, shaping bone or antler pressure flakers, making hoops for drums or fish nets, shaping soapstone, sharpening awls for sewing buckskin, making ritual items, and more. Use-wear and residue analysis should be able to distinguish some of the activities in which these tools were used.

Scrapers composed another 5–15 percent of the assemblages, and again are very versatile tools made mainly on flakes from block cores, but often a bit larger than utilized flakes. They were probably used in the same tasks as utilized flakes but for longer periods of time, and were resharpened on a number of occasions. Thus scrapers probably indicate more prolonged and involved activities such as making spears or spearthrowers, making hoops for drums or fishnets, or shaping soapstone.

What we call minimally used, expedient scrapers were minimally retouched and difficult to distinguish from intensively used utilized flakes. They were similar to both and probably used for the same range of activities. They usually constituted another 10 percent of the housepit assemblages.

Notches, on the other hand, were probably used for a narrower range of tasks involving the sharpening or shaving of narrow diameter shafts or points in wood or bone like spears, arrows, awls, or flakers. Notches were typically made on flakes from block cores and represented 5–10 percent of housepit assemblages.

End scrapers and miscellaneous tool types were also usually made from block core flakes and usually constituted another 5–10 percent of many household assemblages.

Scheduling Tasks and Stone Use

All in all, block core reduction flakes were used for about 50–70 percent of the retouched tool assemblages from housepits. This strong emphasis on expedient production and use of flakes makes good design sense in maintaining great flexibility in producing flakes for diverse and unpredictable task needs involving the removal of small amounts of the wood or bone materials being worked, especially given strong constraints on the amount of raw material available for flake production. It could be that with long stretches of hibernation-like down time people could not clearly plan when they would need to repair a basket or spear or arrow. But whatever the causal factor, the expedient reduction of block cores became a generally adopted strategy of increasingly sedentary hunter-gatherers and horticulturalists in many parts of the world.

At Keatley Creek it seems clear that the effective completion of all the tasks in housepits depended on fairly robust but sharp tool edges to solve the main problem of how to shape hard materials into pointed implements or other shapes, or—in the case of end scrapers—how to create useful edges for scraping hides. Cryptocrystalline and fine-grained stones were sought to achieve these tasks most effectively. Given the wide variety of people who needed to sharpen wood or bone/antler implements, it is understandable why the main reduction strategy required minimal skill. The tasks in which most of these flakes could have been used include activities traditionally carried out by either men or women: making spears, bows, arrows, hoops for fishing, and ritual items for men; hide scraping, sewing, and basket making for women.

Bifacial Reduction

At the opposite end of the design spectrum, bifacial reduction constituted a carefully planned strategy for making flakes, as well as in the production of a specific versatile, multifunctional core tool: the bifacial knife—perhaps an early prototype of the pocket knife. The design logic for bifacial knives appears much the same as the Acheulian bifaces discussed in previous chapters; that is, the mobility constraints of pursuit hunting favored carrying the lightest, least cumbersome tools possible. This in turn favored multifunctional tools that could be used for resharpening/repairing spears or bows and arrows, cutting through skin and butchering, making cordage and fire drills, and undertaking other hunting-related tasks. Bifaces and the flakes from them formed an excellent design solution for these hunting foray constraints, one that was repeatedly adopted by hunters on most continents.

Biface Taphonomy

At Keatley Creek broken biface fragments—and on very rare occasions, whole bifaces or biface stubs—only constituted about 5 percent or less of most housepit retouched tool assemblages. Billet debitage flakes were present in about the same frequencies as biface fragments and were especially concentrated in the bedding areas around the periphery of the housepit floors. So if bifaces were used in hunting contexts, why do they show up taphonomically in housepits? Ordinarily, one would expect bifaces to be used (and broken) primarily on hunting forays, or perhaps even at fishing camps if they were used to butcher fish. At first glance most excavators would usually assume that broken pieces of bifaces and their billet thinning flakes were from people using and resharpening bifaces in pithouses. If so, it would seem that people were removing billet flakes from bifaces (i.e., knapping) in these bedding areas, or that they were actually using billet flakes in these areas.

However, what if billet flakes and pieces of broken bifaces from winter hunting camps were saved by hunters (or fishers) due to the shortage of raw materials back at the pithouse village? When the hunters returned to the winter pithouses, they could have carried and placed the broken biface pieces and billet flakes in their personal spaces where they slept—very possibly under sleeping platforms as convenient storage places. Many billet flakes were retouched and used and the broken edges of many pieces of bifaces were also used. This is most parsimoniously explained in terms of saving and recycling. Alternatively, as Robert Kelly (following Lewis Binford) has argued, gearing up and replacing broken tools for hunting trips is likely to have taken place at residential camps, which may be why these items are found in residences rather than mainly at hunting sites. I am not sure this is a complete explanation.

Biface Advantages

In any case (as discussed in Chapter 5), the creation of bifaces through bifacial reduction makes most sense in terms of material and time design constraints in hunting and fishing tasks—as well as the need for very sharp-edged, low-angled cutting flakes. Bifaces were certainly very maintainable, but to what extent they were also reliable should be reassessed. The presence of these tools and reduction strategies in winter housepits testifies to the importance of these activities for residents, even if these tools and reduction strategies were not systematically used in or around housepits, but only made and stored there (as Binford has suggested for logistical base camps).

In terms of the billet flakes produced by bifacial reduction, many of these could have been used for cutting through hides until dull—at which point they could simply have been replaced by the removal of another thinning flake from the biface. Alternatively, some of them could have been resharpened using expedient invasive pressure retouch. As explained in Chapter 4, only by using pressure flaking could a low, sharp edge angle be maintained over several resharpenings. Expedient knives constituted about 10 percent of the assemblages in housepits, so their use (or storage) was common at housepits but their presence is far from representing a dominant activity. Interestingly, almost half of the expedient knives recovered at Keatley Creek were made on billet flakes, which makes sense if they were serving the same function as unre-touched billet flakes. As with unretouched billet flakes, retouched expedient knives may have been saved during forays and brought back to the pithouses for future use, although they may also have been used—or possibly manufactured—at the pithouses for cutting hides and making buckskin clothes.

Prestige Bifaces

The use and role of expedient knives needs to be investigated further, especially since concave edges occur with some frequency on these pieces (an unusual shape for cutting things, but possibly good for removing scales from fish skin). Expedient knives are also often made on primary flakes from block cores, which might not be expected to occur on hunting forays even though this still would be possible—especially if some hunters were not adept at bifacial reduction. In any event, it seems fairly certain that expedient knives (even those made on block core flakes) were used for cutting some kind of flexible material like thick skin with hair, tough skins of fish, meat, or tanned hides.

Aside from being practical solutions to the needs and constraints of the time, bifaces at Keatley Creek could also sometimes be—and certainly sometimes were—used as prestige items. I excavated a meat-roasting pit in an area of the site that I think was used for rituals. At the very bottom of the pit, under layers of bone and charcoal, were two complete bifaces carefully arranged horizontally. One of them was a totally unique, crescent-shaped biface of very fine craftsmanship that was clearly a highly unusual item of some importance (Figure 8.2). The other was a more ordinary biface. We have also recovered pieces of bifaces made out of stunning raw materials like chalcedony, which must have been prized prestige possessions—similar to the obsidian wealth bifaces used in California (see Figure 5.10).

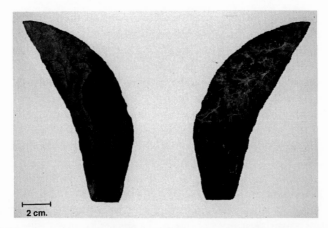

2 cm.

Figure 8.2. One of the most intriguing artifacts recovered in the excavations at Keatley Creek was this crescent biface found carefully laid at the bottom of a meat-roasting pit, next to what has been interpreted as a ritual structure.

Bipolar Reduction

There are two types of bipolar reduction represented at Keatley Creek. One is for producing thin, sharp flakes from cores too small to flake by direct percussion; the other is for the production of large cobble spalls. Flakes from these two types were clearly used in different tasks and the bipolar strategy was adopted for different purposes, so they should not be lumped together in analysis.

Bipolar Flake Production

The first type of bipolar reduction at Keatley Creek seems to have been frequently used on exhausted block cores that were too small to easily remove further flakes. Alternatively, given the extent of residual cortex, there are some instances where small pieces of raw material seem to have been reduced from the beginning using bipolar reduction. In addition, pieces of broken bifaces or other large flake tools were sometimes recycled to produce small cutting flakes by using bipolar reduction. All these cases together comprised about 5 percent of housepit assemblages, which makes sense as an alternate solution to the block core strategy for occasionally producing small flakes with a sharp edge or two when raw material was limited and needed to be conserved.

Bipolar Spall Production

The second type of bipolar reduction was used to produce large cobble spalls that were usually of quartzite with medium- or even large-grain characteristics (Figure 8.3). While they were definitely present at Keatley Creek, they were not common—around 1 percent of all assemblages. Ethnographically, cobble spalls were used in this region to deal with the problem of creating tools for the hard work of stretching, abrading, and softening hides in which considerable force was used. A large round edge was an optimal solution for applying pressure to the hides as they dried in order to avoid punching through the hide, which could happen with tools that were too pointed. Similarly, the coarse grain of the stone minimized any danger of cutting through the hides on stretching frames while still enabling workers to abrade any remaining bits of meat, fat, or membrane. Hafted spall tools constituted one very good solution (among several) for stretching the hide so that it became soft.

The design question is why such hafted spall scrapers were better solutions than using blunt sticks, block-shaped abrading stones, or a number of other solutions to achieve the desired results of soft, pliable, clean buckskin production. For a full analysis, it still needs to be determined how many hides would be needed by a family per year for clothing or other needs, how many hides a spall scraper could process over its lifetime (probably a lot), how many hides might have been brought back from the summer mountain hunts for processing during winters, how many hides were processed into buckskin in the mountains, and how many hides could have been processed using alternative types of tools. Answering these questions entail a good deal of sophisticated research.

Given that hafted spall tools had some clear advantages, the next problem was how to produce such spalls. Direct percussion is often difficult to use on round cobbles, as you may have discovered in the exer-

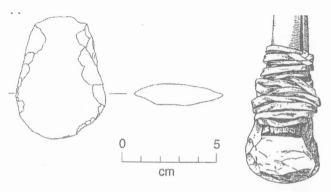

Figure 8.3. One of the spall tools from the Keatley Creek site (illustration by Suzanne Villeneuve) compared with a hafted ethnographic specimen recorded by James Teit (1900, p. 185, Figure 127). See also Figure 3.3.

cise in Chapter 1. It also tends to produce short flakes rather than the large sizes sought by hideworkers. However, river-rounded cobbles of quartzite can be effectively and more easily split by using bipolar percussion, sometimes with just a persistent tapping using a good-sized hammerstone—a technique used by many hideworking women. Alternatively, rounded cobbles can be set on a suitable anvil and held upright by piling dirt around them. It is then possible to throw a large block of stone vertically at the top of the cobble in order to split it. Thus there are minimal skill constraints. Moreover, quartzite cobbles are fairly common occurrences in streambeds and riverbeds in the British Columbian interior and availability is not usually much of an issue.

Pressure Reduction

Pressure flaking used to reduce a piece of stone and shape it (rather than simply resharpening it, as with expedient knives) was employed at Keatley Creek primarily to shape projectile points. Projectile points, which were usually found in a broken state, made up about 5 percent of most housepit assemblages. This reflects a fairly important component in the winter resource economy, matched by a similar frequency of biface fragments. Presumably, broken projectile points came back from winter hunting forays still attached to spear or arrow shafts, or still lodged in some of the joints of meat brought back.

Drills were also shaped using pressure flaking, as were a number of curious eccentrics that appear to have been shaped into unusual—sometimes zoomorphic—outlines for unknown purposes. They may have been considered prestige items, together with a number of simple ground stone pendants. Drills were rare (around 1 percent) and eccentrics constituted less than 0.1 percent of the assemblage.

Grinding Reduction

Although ground stone cutting tools are not chipped stone, they are usually included in lithic analyses of chipped stone. Ground stone chopping tools replaced chipped stone chopping tools, which largely dropped out of the assemblages as a result. So a brief mention about them will be made here.

Nephite Adzes

There are very few chipped stone adzes at Keatley Creek. These are made of a tough material that is resistant to chipping—quartzite—and were probably used by individuals who could not afford to make, borrow, or rent a nephrite adze. Similarly, there are only a very few pieces of nephrite adzes at the site (Figure 8.4). Nephrite is visually and mechanically indistinguishable from jade and occurs in the streambeds near Lillooet, about twenty kilometers from Keatley Creek. Nephrite is resistant to flaking; it is very tough and cannot be flaked in any controlled fashion. To make tools with it, grinding must be used. Based on the traditional Chinese method of grinding jade, it takes about one hour to grind down one millimeter of jade. Making nephrite adzes was therefore extremely labor-intensive, perhaps only made practical by the use of slave labor. Nephrite adzes were also extremely valuable.

While there can be little doubt that nephrite adzes were used intensively to fell and cut to size the many trees needed to build pithouses, it would be impossible to determine this from the few pieces of adzes found at the site. Due to their great value, most of these tools were probably buried with their owners or passed on to others when their owners died. Nephrite adzes were not merely practical tools, but they were also prestige items—a rare combination that made sense in both domains.

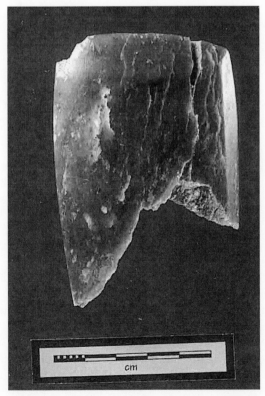

Figure 8.4. A broken ground stone nephrite adze from the Keatley Creek site.

Ideological Considerations

There may also have been ideological factors involved in choosing nephrite for tools, as there were in China and Mesoamerica. Nephrite, like jade, has a beautiful green luster to it when ground and polished, and green may well have been imbued with symbolic importance—especially in dry environments like the Mid-Fraser Valley where cactus and sagebrush are common. Such green items could be used as symbols of spiritual connections and resultant wealth. These associations could in turn be used as claims for supernaturally sanctioned inequalities and socioeconomic hierarchies, which were well documented ethnographically in the area. In fact, unusually long (and non-functional) nephrite adzes must have been explicitly used as displays of prestige and wealth.

Ground Adze Capitalism and Cutting Needs

In addition, these adzes are probably one of the first instances of control over the technological means of production—a feature usually associated with capitalism. There can be little doubt of their high value or that only some families would have owned them. Other families would have had to borrow or rent the adzes to build houses, or else content themselves with much simpler shelters that could be constructed with chipped stone adzes (like the rare examples that occurred at Keatley Creek).

Based on the ethnographic illustrations of pithouses (Figure 8.5) by George Dawson and James Teit, it can be estimated that construction of an average-sized pithouse required about 312 logs (24 large logs, 44 medium-sized logs, and 244 smaller logs) plus poles for sleeping platforms, covering cache pits, and many other purposes like constructing log ladders, deer fences, elevated storage platforms, fishing platforms, hoops for fishing nets, drying racks, hunting equipment, obtaining tree bark and cambium, and making wood sculptures. There were well over a hundred pithouses at Keatley Creek, so the magnitude of the problem of how to cut the wood necessary for all the structural and other technological needs—well over 31,000 logs and poles simply for building pithouse structures at the site—can be appreciated.

From a design perspective, it was the high volume of cutting required for constructing pithouses that made design and economic sense of the substantial amount of labor investment in manufacturing nephrite adzes. Nephrite adzes would never have been made for cutting the few saplings needed to make a simple lean-to shelter or a few spears. Thus the appearance of ground stone cutting tools throughout the Northwest around three thousand years ago makes most sense in terms of the increased cutting requirements engendered by making dugout canoes, substantial house constructions, and fish weirs. Due to their very long

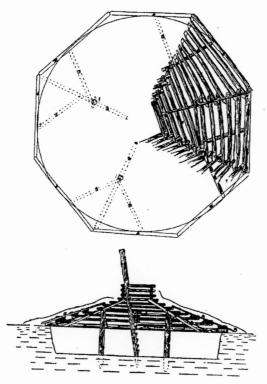

Figure 8.5. An illustration of the construction of an ethnographic pithouse show-ing the large number of wooden beams required for their construction. (From Dawson 1892, p. 13, Figure 3)

active use-lives, nephrite adzes would have also reduced the need for re-stocking chipped stone material suitable for cutting wood, and this would have helped offset the high cost of making the nephrite adzes. The highly valued nephrite tools would certainly have been carried by their owners on all seasonal residential moves, but the overall transport costs were probably far less than those requiring the transport of multi-ple block cores and choppers on such moves.

Raw Material Procurement

Given its local occurrence as cobbles in streambeds or riverbeds, pro-curement cost of the material would not have been excessive. Suitable cobbles might have been collected while fishing or visiting neighboring communities, although finding pieces of nephrite in streambeds is rare and many hours of search time would have been involved. Presumably, anyone finding such material would hoard it as a valued exchange item. In other regions, nephrite—whether as cobbles or manufactured items—

would have been obtained by trade and certainly would have commanded high prices.

Hafting

Creating an effective haft for nephrite adzes would have also required some skill, time, and effort. However, the reduction of trauma to the hands and the ability to use the tool with considerably greater force than a handheld chopping tool would have more than compensated for the time invested in crafting a good haft, especially given the quantities of wooden material that needed to be cut. These tools would have been highly reliable, although not very multifunctional, and there is no indication they were designed for multifunctional tasks. Maintaining sharp cutting edges would have required suitable sharpening stones like sandstone or other flat stones to which sand grit, and preferably sand with corundum grains in it, could be added. We have no evidence of such sharpening stones at Keatley Creek, although they must have existed somewhere.

OTHER STRATEGIES AND COMPARISONS

Curiously, although we know from isotope analyses that the vast majority of protein consumed by prehistoric residents in the region was derived from salmon, and that each individual must have consumed hundreds of salmon every year, we cannot as yet identify any tools specifically associated with the capture or butchering of salmon. These activities were strenuous, tightly time-constrained tasks at the height of the salmon runs. Therefore we would expect some specialized tools to have been used. Whether bifaces, bifacial thinning flakes, expedient knives, or other tools were used for butchering salmon at summer fishing camps by the river cannot be determined from our excavations at winter village sites.

For comparative purposes, and to characterize entire assemblages in a simple fashion, I suggest that once tools are assigned to specific strategies, the proportional contributions of all the strategies to the overall assemblage can be visually portrayed by the simple means of histograms or bar charts—each bar representing a different strategy and its importance in the assemblage.

ADDITIONAL READINGS

Hayden, Brian, Nora Franco, and Jim Spafford. 2000. Keatley Creek Lithic Strategies and Design. In *The Ancient Past of Keatley Creek, Vol. 1:*

Taphonomy, edited by Brian Hayden (pp. 185–212). Archaeology Press, Simon Fraser University, Burnaby, British Columbia, Canada. A more systematic and complete analysis of the Keatley Creek assemblage than the overview we published in 1996.

Parry, William J., and Kelly, Robert L. 1987. Expedient Core Technology and Sedentism. In *The Organization of Core Technology*, edited by Jay K. Johnson and Carol A. Morrow (pp. 285–304). Westview Press, Boulder, Colorado. This is one of the first articles to bring the correspondence between sedentism and expedient core reduction to the attention of archaeologists. The assemblage at Keatley Creek certainly fits the model and causal reasons proposed by Parry and Kelly.

Spafford, Jim. 2000. Socioeconomic Inference from Floor Distributions of Lithics at Keatley Creek and Comparison of Lithic Assemblages from All Excavated and Tested Housepits at the Keatley Creek Site. In *The Ancient Past of Keatley Creek, Vol. 2: Socioeconomy*, edited by Brian Hayden (pp. 167–178). Archaeology Press, Simon Fraser University, Burnaby, British Columbia, Canada. Spafford's analysis of the distribution of stone tool types across housepit floors is an excellent example of how lithics can be used to infer family hearth groups, sexual division of labor, activity areas, prestige areas, and storage areas. His overall comparison of assemblages from the site clearly shows the main tendencies, including strong redundant patterning between housepits.

CHAPTER 9

PRECEPTS AND PROSPECTS

We have covered a great deal about lithics in relatively few pages. However, I think you will find that most of the critical issues have at least been introduced and that you have acquired sufficient orientation to embark on much more in-depth understanding of lithic technology if you choose to do so.

GETTING ORIENTED

I have tried to convey eight important points in this primer.

(1) Read the ethnographies for insights into how stone tools were made and used.

(2) Experiment by yourself in using stone tools to solve basic problems that would have confronted hunter-gatherers or other groups you deal with. Do some stone knapping yourself.

(3) Look at the stone tools from the perspective of the users and try to understand their constraints and the solutions that made the most sense to them. In this quest I recommend design theory as the most useful perspective.

(4) In analyzing flake tools, find out where the point of impact was, examine all six sides of the flake, and determine what was done to the flake after it was struck from the core.

(5) Pay attention to flake modifications that are often ignored by other analysts such as notches, denticulates, expedient knives, bipolar cores, *pièces esquillées*, intentional breaks, r-billet flakes, and various other flake tools that may have been overlooked. Stay alert to new patterns of flake modification or the unusual occurrence of some unmodified types of flakes. Become familiar with the unusual or unique types of stone tools found in the region where you work.

137

(6) Look at the various types of debitage related to different reduction strategies and the modified flake tools to see what reduction strategies were used. Try to figure out why different reduction strategies were preferred.

(7) Pay special attention to distinguishing between bipolar cores and medial sections of broken bifaces. Also, be sure to identify r-billet flakes as grievous flaking mistakes rather than fragments of broken bifaces.

(8) Experiment with trampled versus used flake edges. See how accurate you are in identifying each. There will always be some overlap and some percentage of errors. The main issue is how much overlap there is.

In addition to these ways of approaching lithic analysis, I would urge any serious student of stone technology to take advantage of every opportunity possible to visit traditional communities that use or once used stone technologies. We desperately need more ethnographic observations on the traditional use of all stone tools, whether chipped or ground. You may be able to develop research focused on groups that are still known to use stone tools. But serendipitous opportunities sometimes pop up in the most unexpected situations—for example, the metate maker with whom I worked in Guatemala, the women who still use stone spall tools in northern British Columbia, or the use of bipolar reduction to make sharp flakes for scarification rituals in East Africa.

I have been unusually fortunate in finding people who grew up using stone tools in traditional communities. But even in situations where such people no longer exist, it is sometimes still possible to study how substitute materials like metals are used and modified. For instance, in Guatemala we found that many people broke glass bottles and used the shards for hide scraping and smoothing wooden handles. I have seen similar use of glass in tribal villages in Southeast Asia. And even where such substitutes don't exist, it is still useful to observe the kinds of traditional tasks in which metal cutting tools are used in order to infer the tasks in which stone tools would have been used prehistorically. This is an approach that I also used in the Maya Highlands.

PROSPECTS

Going through an entire program of training in lithic analysis is really a lifelong undertaking in experimenting with materials and tasks and reading about all the relevant factors. The experiential aspect is fun and engaging. Together with the background research, the lithic quest is like fitting together pieces of a puzzle until a coherent picture emerges. In approaching lithic analysis this way, you not only gain analytical skills for dealing with many different materials in prehistoric assemblages, but you gain a wide range of practical and analytical skills that can potentially be useful in a variety of circumstances or conditions. Perhaps more importantly, you gain a much more fundamental and satisfying understanding of how the world works.

There are a fairly limited number of things that can be done to and with a piece of stone via chipping it; however, the way those things are expressed varies according to core or flake topography, material, and stone knapping skills and tools. It is enormously gratifying to be able to take an artifact of chipped stone and be able to tell how it was produced, what was done to it, what it might have been used for, and perhaps something of its design history or its life story.

Research Constraints

All this being said, I also feel it necessary to warn students of lithic technology that the analysis of stone tools can be exhausting, especially when dealing with large numbers of stone artifacts (often thousands, tens of thousands, or hundreds of thousands of items). If analyses require making numerous quantifiable and qualitative observations on each item, the task can become overwhelming. However, this is true of the analysis of many kinds of archaeological remains, including faunal and botanical remains. It is frequently necessary to take some measurements or make some qualitative observations, but these should be kept to a minimum. The size of many assemblages is usually the most daunting aspect of analysis. There are several ways of dealing with this to make it more manageable.

(1) *Size.* As the size of objects decreases, the number of pieces you have to deal with increases, usually in a logarithmic fashion. Therefore sorting materials by size will enable you to only treat the size categories of interest to you in some detail (e.g., only artifact size categories greater than 2–3 centimeters). For small samples of debitage, sorting pieces by size can be done quickly using a piece of graph paper gridded into appropriately sized boxes. For larger samples this can be done with a set of graduated geological sieves. Anything smaller than two centimeters can simply be weighed or counted. Usually, the only objects smaller than two centimeters that are easily recognizable are microblades, pressure flakes, and beads. Samples can be quickly scanned for these or other special small items and they can be treated separately.

(2) *Sampling.* Sampling can be used in many circumstances. In plow zones or sites with large uniform strata, not every sample needs to be analyzed in detail. As long as you have a representative sample from every important strata, the rest of the samples from that strata can often be ignored, although they should be scanned for unusual pieces or types of special interest. If there are good reasons to think there may be spatial

patterning across surfaces, it may be necessary to adapt stratified sampling strategies to investigate each area of interest.

(3) *Focus.* It is possible to focus on restricted aspects of assemblages in order to address specific questions without doing a comprehensive examination of everything and all potentially important features of stone tools. Remember, the number of observations that can be made on a single stone tool are potentially unlimited, especially if relationships to other artifactual objects are taken into account. You simply cannot record all possible observations on artifacts. You always have to select the observations you make with specific purposes in mind. What observations are you going to choose and for what purposes? The purposes can be narrowed down to aspects like raw material, degree of material transport (e.g., how much cortex occurs on flakes), degree of curation or personal gear, use-lives of specific tool types, reduction strategies used or dominant, occurrence of prestige items, or many other specific questions.

(4) *Help.* Find additional qualified help and make sure there are enough funds to cover all the analysis that is being requested.

If you decide to pursue the analysis of stone tools despite these drawbacks, I wish you an adventurous and rewarding time in the quest to understand what stone tools are and were. Your decision can lead to a very fulfilling life designed for understanding stone tools, but it needs to be tempered with the realistic constraints of time, resources, and balance of other life aspects. Happy knapping.

ADDITIONAL READING

Deal, Michael, and Brian Hayden. 1987. The Persistence of Pre-Columbian Lithic Technology in the Form of Glassworking. In *Lithic Studies Among the Contemporary Highland Maya*, edited by Brian Hayden, pp. 235–331. University of Arizona Press, Tucson. Both this and the preceding and subsequent chapters demonstrate the unexpected type of information that can be obtained in modern-day traditional communities for helping to understand lithic assemblages. The modern breaking of bottles in order to use glass fragments for scraping tool handles, hides, and making incisions has obvious parallels for stone tools.

SOURCES FOR IMAGES

Cover. A finely crafted sacrificial bifacial knife recovered from the Sacred Cenote at Chichen Itza. Peabody Museum Expedition, E. H. Thompson, Director, 1907–1910. Image © President and Fellows of Harvard College, Peabody Museum of Archaeology and Ethnology, 10–71–20/C6755.

Figure 2.1. From "Practical and Prestige Technologies: The Evolution of Material Systems" by Brian Hayden, *Journal of Archaeological Method and Theory*, 5, 1998, pp. 1–55.

Figures 3.2 and 3.5. From *Blue Mountain Buckskin: A Working Manual–Dry-Scrape Brain-Tan* by Jim Riggs, self-published, 1980.

Figure 3.3. From *The Thompson Indians of British Columbia* by James Alexander Teit, American Museum of Natural History, 1900.

Figure 4.2. From *Archaeology: The Science of Once and Future Things* by Brian Hayden, W. H. Freeman, 1993.

Figures 4.4 and 4.5. From "Stone Implement Making Among the Nakako, Ngadadjara, and Pitjandjara of the Great Western Desert" by Norman Tindale, *Records of the South Australian Museum*, 15, 1965, pp. 131–164.

Figures 4.7, 4.9 (left), 4.13, 4.16, and 4.18. From *Typologie du Paléolithique Ancien et Moyen* by François Bordes, Delmas, 1961.

Figures 4.9 (right), 4.10, and 5.6. From "Typology" by Brian Hayden and Jim Spafford, in *The Ancient Past of Keatley Creek, Vol. 3: Excavations and Artifacts*, edited by Brian Hayden and Jim Spafford, Archaeology Press, 2000, pp. 1–34.

Figures 5.3 and 5.10. From *Life and Culture of the Hupa* by Pliny Earle Goddard, University of California Press, 1903.

Figures 5.7 and 5.8. From "Whither the Billet Flake?" by Brian Hayden and W. Karl Hutchings, in *Experiments in Lithic Technology*, edited by Daniel S. Amick and Raymond P. Mauldin, British Archaeological Reports No. 528, 1989, pp. 235–257.

Figure 5.11. From *Handbook of the Indians of California* by A. L. Kroeber, Government Printing Office, 1925.

Figure 6.1. From "Technological Organization and Settlement Mobility" by Michael Shott, *Journal of Anthropological Research*, 42, 1986, pp. 15–51.

Figure 8.5. From *Notes on the Shuswap People of British Columbia* by George Dawson, Proceedings and Transactions of the Royal Society of Canada No. 9, 1892.

GLOSSARY

adze: A woodcutting tool hafted and used like a garden hoe.

atlatl **or spearthrower:** Usually, a wooden shaft used as an extension of the arm to propel spears with more force—the spear being seated at the end of the shaft on a hook or in a depression.

backing: Flakes abruptly removed along the edge of a flake or blade, usually to blunt the edge for prehension or to create a thick edge suitable for hafting with mastic.

bedding plane: A preferential line of fracture in stones created by the deposition of successive layers of sediment.

biface: A core tool created by bifacial reduction using soft hammers and typically exhibiting a lenticular cross-section. Bifaces do not include projectile points made by pressure flaking.

billet: A soft hammer usually made of antler or hard wood used in bifacial reduction.

billet flake: A flake removed from a biface with a soft hammer or billet, typically having a very small platform remnant from which it expands—being very thin—and having a curved longitudinal cross-section.

blade: Technically any flake over twice as long as it is wide, however usually reserved for intentionally produced elongated removals from specially prepared cores for blade production. Does not include "bifaces" as defined above.

brittleness: A property of stones that makes their edges susceptible to shattering and breakage when used or misused.

buckskin: A type of leather characterized by its softness. Buckskin is produced by removing the upper hair layers of skin with follicles and the lower layer of membrane, followed by stretching as the skin dries after tanning in order to soften it.

bulb of percussion: A raised, partial cone area formed directly under the point of impact of a hard hammer.

burin: A flake modified by holding the flake vertically with an edge oriented toward the knapper and removing a single long "spall" along one edge.

chert: A sedimentary rock composed of microcrystalline or cryptocrystalline quartz. Most chert is microcrystalline quartz with minor chalcedony and sometimes opal, but cherts range from nearly pure opal to nearly pure quartz. Purity ranges from 99 percent silica to less than 65 percent. Synonymous with "flint".

chopper: A core tool with one or more edges unifacially or bifacially flaked by hard hammer percussion to create an edge suitable for cutting into wood or similar materials.

cobble: According to the Wentworth scale, any stone 64–256 millimeters in size.

composite tool: Any hafted tool, especially those with two or more individual stone elements such as hafted knives with multiple flakes along the cutting edge.

conchoidal fracture: A cone-shaped fracture (like flakes produced by BB pellets fired onto plate glass) or a fracture forming any part of a cone, as with hard hammer flake removals from vitreous or cryptocrystalline rocks.

core: A piece of stone from which flakes are removed.

cortex: The weathered, discolored, outside "rind" of a block or a core, or its remnants on flakes.

crested blade: The first blade struck from a boat-shaped blade core with the striking platform represented by the deck of the boat, and the keel (prow to the water) representing the crested blade.

cryptocrystalline: A rock that has a crystalline structure visible only when magnified.

curation: Keeping a tool for future use.

dart: Short for "long dart," or a short spear used with a spearthrower.

debitage: Unwanted stone waste products from reducing cores to make useful tools.

denticulate: A series of aligned notches on one or more edges of a flake; in French usage (*denticulé*), any flake with more than one notch anywhere.

diversity: The number of different tool types in an assemblage.

dorsal face: The face of a flake that was on the outside of the core before removal.

eccentric: A pressure-flaked piece of stone without an obvious practical function, often in the form of an animal, bird, or organic shape.

edge angle: The angle formed by the ventral and dorsal (or retouched) faces of a flake or tool.

endscraper or *grattoir*: A flake with very regular retouch forming a convex working edge, from 1–3 centimeters wide, usually on elongated flakes or blades and designed for scraping animal hides.

endoderm: The lowest layer of skin that includes the inner membrane of skin.

epiderm: The top layer, or "grain," of skin containing hair and follicles.

ethnoarchaeology: The study of traditional (pre-industrial) societies in order to understand and interpret archaeological remains.

exotics: Nonlocal stone materials from sources farther away than one day's travel.

expedient knife: A sharp, low-angled (< 55 degrees) flake that has been expediently resharpened by pressure flaking forming a series of small, uniform, continuous invasive flake removals on one or more edges.

fillet: A thin slice of meat or fish often made for drying and storing.

fissure: A linear fracture feature that radiates out from the point of impact like spokes from a wheel hub.

flake: A piece of stone intentionally detached from a core of raw material with conchoidal fracture.

flexibility: A stone tool designed to undergo varying numbers of functional transformations.

flint: See "chert."

foreshaft: A piece of hard wood, bone, or antler attached at the front end of a projectile to give weight and to serve for the attachment of the head.

glass: Any type of stone-like material lacking a crystal structure.

grattoir: See "endscraper."

half-moon break: A small concave or crescent-shaped fracture with a "break" initiation and abrupt termination forming a completely right-angled fracture termination. Typically formed on thin edges of flakes.

handaxe: A core tool with a relatively thick lenticular cross-section produced by bifacial reduction, characterizing the Acheulian tradition.

hard hammer: A hammerstone that produces conchoidal fractures.

heat treatment: Heating cryptocrystalline materials sufficiently to anneal crystal structures so that pressure flakes can be more easily removed.

housepit: The depression left by a residential structure that was partly dug into the ground and roofed.

inverse retouch: Retouch in which retouch flakes are removed from a flake's ventral face.

Kombewa: An unusual technique in which a flake is produced with two bulbar faces by refashioning the striking platform of a large flake to remove another smaller flake from the bulbar area. The resulting flake has a circular shape and very sharp edges around the entire periphery.

laurel leaf: A thin bipointed biface produced in the Solutrean culture.

lenticular: A lens-shaped (concave-convex), cross-section.

Levallois: A technique of producing a large flake with low-angled edges around its entire periphery by removing it from the domed surface of a core.

maintainability: The capacity of a tool to be easily and quickly repaired or resharpened.

microblade: In the French tradition, a blade that is less than twelve millimeters in width. In Eastern Asia and North America, widths are typically less than six millimeters.

microlith: Tools usually made from microblades and backed.

multifunctionality: Indications that a tool was used for more than one purpose—that is, with more than one kind of retouch or use-wear.

nephrite: A stone almost identical with jade but having a slightly different chemical composition. It is tough and dense and cannot be flaked, but must be ground.

normal retouch: Retouch in which retouch flakes are removed from a flake's dorsal face.

obsidian: A natural glass from volcanic ejections that have cooled very rapidly preventing crystal formation.

patina: Discoloration or alteration of the fractured surface of a flaked stone due to weathering.

pebble: In the Wentworth scale, a stone 4–64 millimeters in size.

percussor: An object used to remove flakes from cores in a percussive manner, including hammerstones and billets.

pièce esquillée: A flake or similar piece of stone used as a wedge to split wood or antler. The *pièce* typically exhibits small bipolar and bifacial flaking or crushing on the working edges.

pithouse: See "housepit."

plane of cleavage: The preferential direction of fracture that some crystals exhibit due to their crystalline structure—for example, micas and salt crystals.

potlid: A small, round, bowl-like fracture that pops off the surface of cryptocrystalline rocks due to heating.

pressure flake: A flake removed by pressing onto the edge of a flake or core, either with a handheld flaker or a chest press.

quartzite: A metamorphic rock composed of consolidated quartz grains.

r-billet flake: A flake removed from a biface by a billet that has mistakenly struck too far into the biface, thereby removing a large section of the edge. R-billet flakes exhibit large, thick striking platforms and are fairly short.

reliable: A tool that won't break or fail when being used.

ring of percussion: See "undulations."

scraper: A flake tool exhibiting continuous, semi-abrupt retouch (55–80 degree edge angles) along one or more margins.

soft hammer: A percussor of antler, wood, or some soft stones, capable of removing billet flakes.

solifluction: Lateral flow movement of frozen ground due to melting.

spearthrower: See *atlatl.*

step fracture: A flake or retouch with a right-angled termination.

toughness: The capacity of a material to resist fracture.

trachydacite: An extrusive igneous rock composed mostly of feldspar but enriched with silica. It is usually fine grained, formed by the rapid cooling of lava.

truncation: A flake with abrupt retouch (circa 90 degrees) at its distal end.

typology: The classification of objects or organisms in order to study features of theoretical interest.

undulations: Ripples on the ventral surface of flakes that originate at the point of percussion and spread outward like ripples from a stone dropped in water.

use-wear: Damage on the edge of a tool created by use—especially crushing, rounding, polishing, striating, and fracturing.

ventral ripples/undulations/rings of percussion: See "undulations."

vitreous: Glassy